Border Voices

The San Diego Celebration of Poetry & Music

THE Seventh Annual
Anthology of Poetry
by Major Poets and
San Diego Students
2000

ISBN 0-9640275-6-9

Copyright 2000 by Jack Webb
San Diego, California

All rights reserved. No part of this work may be reproduced or transmitted in any form by any means, except as may be expressly permitted by the 1976 Copyright Act or in writing by the publisher. Requests for such permission should be addressed to:

Jack Webb
P.O. Box 120191
San Diego, CA 92112-0191

Art Director: Leslie L.J. Reilly,
Community Relations
The San Diego Union-Tribune

Layout: Celia Sigmon

Production: Chris Dickerson

Cover Illustration: Leslie L.J. Reilly

Cover Poem: "Writing Is Digging" by Becky Espinosa, Grade 7, Pauma School

Biographies of featured poets: Jack Webb

Photo Credits: Photo of Martín Espada by Paul Shoul; photo of Mark Strand – © Emily Mott; photo of Genny Lim by Bob Hsiang; Photo of Sharon Olds by David Bartolomi.

Best Buds / Justine Cori Keovoravongsa
Grade 4 / Canyon View Elementary

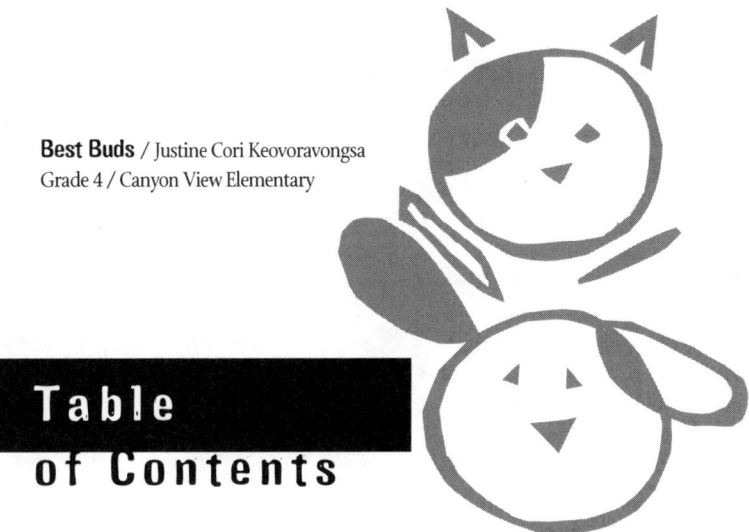

Table of Contents

Sarah Lambert, "Empty"	34
Jessica Trail, "The Burned Doll"	35
Julian Goodin, "Nocturnal City"	36
Devon Galindo, "Gridlock Games"	37
Zhengkan Wang, "A Simple Crystal Memory"	38
Carolyn Pratt, "My Mother's Ring"	39
Spencer Reynolds, "Work"	40
Kassy Lee, "The Power Of My Culture"	41
Alyssia Veiga, "I'm a Fire-Breathing Dragon"	42
Rob Low, "Dragon Boy"	43
Qiana Neff, "A Window on Logan"	44
Matt Kelly, "My Brother's Tempo"	46
Reina Marie Valadez, "Song Wish"	47
Matt Lutes, "The Wounded Deer"	48
Alexis Bittar, "Sticky History"	48
Kota Oe, "Deer"	49
Jessica Kondrick, "Night"	50
Febiana Hernandez, "Pearl Talk"	51
David Taing, "I Am"	51
Jordan Laris Cohen, "Spiritual Memories"	52
Sibel Güner, "Everlasting Journey"	53
Geoff Livingston, "Dad"	54
Carson Kemp, "Ear Hunt"	55
Eyal Florentin, "I Hate Book Reports"	56

Jeff Liao, "Jump Word"	57
Josh Peterson, "My Writing"	57
Caitlin Morrow, "Silent Wolf"	58
Julianne Golingan, "If I Were a Hippity Hoppity Green Frog"	59
Sam Sundos, "Car Cemetery"	60
Ryan Beyer, "Road Kill"	61
Tracy Burnett, "Wondrous Things I Have Yet to Understand"	62
John Freeman, "My Eye That's Fly"	63
Vanessa Sanchez, "Considering the Spiders"	64
Danielle Kleinstuber, "Black Widow"	65
Katie Reynolds, "April Fools"	66
Meredith Snapp, "To a Mouse"	67
Rachel Dennis, "Morning Madness"	68
Miguel Urcino, "Morning"	69
Russ Kreeger, "Gray Breath"	69
Ryan Garcia, "The Art of Sky"	70
Karli Kroeker, "Cloud Laugh"	71
Daren Rodhouse, "If I Were a Baseball"	72
Mohamed Iman, "Old White Shoe"	73
Johnny Thongkham, "Halloween Magic"	73
Karen Kim, "A Portrayal of Memories"	74
Spencer Amansec, "Pearl of the Oriental Sea"	77
Becky Espinosa, "Writing Is Digging"	78
Mark Dy, "What If?"	78
Mackenzie Maher, "Tsunami"	79
Jill Brooks, "Sorrow"	80
Kristopher Bognot, "What Am I?"	81
Andres Villa, "Diving Deep"	81
Erin Dawson, "Wings That Won't Fly"	82
Mona Safi, "Stoplight Reflected"	83
Beth Ann Ahlgren, "The Ocean Side"	84
Sarah Ball, "Marian Anderson"	85
Abel Marquez, "Black"	86
Jessica Tiu, "Purple"	86
Margaret Stenchion, "I Am"	87
Alex Cossio, "Listening to the Wind"	88
Lance Moore, "The Tiger's Dream"	89
Mina Khavari, "Tiger Sky"	89
Jasmine Pikes, "My Mom, So Many Things"	90
Steven Nava, "Big Shiny Plates"	91

Midnight Slumber / Karen Lopez
Grade 10 / Morse High

Ronald Reza, "My Tia's Kitchen"	91
Taylor Waldenmaier, "The Oldest Rock I Ever Met"	92
Jacob Peterson, "Old Man"	92
Norma Resendiz, "Globe"	93
Mary Ann Gaudreault, "Beneath the Tree"	94
Garrison Williams, "Bursting Bees"	95
Rachel Paarman, "Orange Trees"	95
Mackenzie Maher, "Wonder Water"	96
Jose Jauregui, "Samoran Night"	97
Lorraine Munoa, "Twilight"	98
Berenice Ledesma, "Shy"	99
Mia Legaspi-Cavin, "A Bright Yellow Room"	99
Cristobal Garcia, "My Mom's Hands"	100
Claudia Haman, "Beautiful Hands"	101
Destini Digiorgio, "Crazy Cat Girl"	102
Amy Wills, "My Cat"	103
Jimmy Orduno, "Backyard of Books"	104
Masumi Taketomi, "Winter Landscape"	105
Kendall Plant, "The Flying Sneeze"	106
Jeremy Shivick, "Anger"	106
Baneza Aguilar, "Howling"	107
Sarah Shearer, "I Am a Shadow"	108
Akio Mitsunaga, "The Song of Loss"	109
Nicole Flores, "I Believe Beautiful Things"	110
Meryn Beckett, "The Petals of the Rose"	111
Delaney Maher, "If I Were an Ocean"	112
Andrew Stuck, "Misty Bay"	113
Jansen Cudal, "Don't Need No Ketchup or Mayonnaise"	114
Dustin Crawford, "Happiness"	115
Jenny Feng, "Popcorn"	116

Meg Felix, "The Fog's Playground"	117
Lizanne Koch, "The Gift"	118
Jami Heard, "A One-Of-a-Kind Design"	119
Lisa Carbone, "Sadness Is a Million Bee Stings"	120
Carolyn Turner, "Loneliness"	121
Aaron Primm, "Crutches"	122
Melissa Duenas, "The Sea"	123
Erika Palmer, "Piano Joys"	124
Millie Umali, "My Family"	124
Kristen Love, "The Blues"	125
Dallis Fox, "Dancing With My Grandmother"	126
Aurelia Alicia Arroyo, "My Mom's Sewing Room"	127
Jeanette Ramirez, "Watermelon Eyes"	127
Elspeth Miller, "A Kitchen Perfumed With Spices"	128
Phuong Pham, "Spring Day"	129
Nathan Torian, "Silent Hill Nocturne"	130
Jasmine Lopez, "Medicine Bag"	131
Caitlin Sussman, "I Believe"	132
Heather Ann Smith, "The Color of Loneliness"	133
Martin Perez, "The Turtle"	134
Anthony Randall, "If I Were a Caterpillar"	135
Orlando Garcia, "Great-Great-Grandfather"	136
Ian Philip Tapang, "The Oldest Thing in the World"	137
Michiyo Wellington-Oguri, "The Failure"	138
Victoria Ryan, "Frozen in Time"	139
Richard Hess, "Poet-One, Poetry-Nothing"	140
Jorges Vidales, "My Mother Is a Tornado"	142
Michael Haider, "Grandfather"	143
Kimberly Cruikshank, "For the Last Time"	144
Jasmine Mayo, "Jasmine Mayo's Complete Guide to Survival"	145
Christian Banzon, "In the Shadows"	146
Carissa Perkins, "Little Dragon of Sorry Ghosts"	146
Steven Burningham, Mysteries from the Soul"	147
Juan Hernandez, "Space"	148
Kelly Bennett, "Talking Crafts"	149
Scott Linger, "Ode to a Limpet Shell"	149
Sarah Sifton, "Two Worlds"	150
Carly Rask, "Sometimes Rough, Sometimes Mellow"	151
Molly Boyne, "I Saw Andi"	152
Marisa Luber, "Art Gallery"	153
Collier Jones, "Nasty Icky Lima Beans"	154

Gohan / Rolando Herrera
Grade 10 / Crawford High

Erika Rodriquez, "My Brother Looks Like a Snail"	154
John Zhang, "Mike"	155
Salvador Arroyo, "Red Comes from the Heart"	156
Angela Raimondi, "Love's Many Shapes"	157
Danielle Hove, "My Grandma and Grandpa"	157
Shannon Mockler, "Blue Monkey Sipping Soda"	158
Jorge Martinez, "Hate"	159
Monica Navarro, "Blinding Yellow"	160
Alegria Vicencio, "The Spoiling of an Aging Kiwi"	161
Danielle Torre, "The Color of Humiliation"	162
Jenny Meza, "The Way I Like It"	162
Alberto Corona, "Anger"	163
B. B. Villanueva, "My Friend, the Red M&M"	164
Ashlee Corona, "My Busy Home"	165
Graciano Avalos, "Green Fire"	166
Katherine Ramos, "Flower"	167
Justin Scholey, "Toilet"	168
Eric Paarman, "Silver Scales"	169
William Franklin, "The Pomegranate"	169
Allister Caluza, "I Am"	170
Tessa Miller, "Shoelaces in Love"	171
Sandy Chan, "A World of Living Color"	172
Victoria Fonseca, "Rattlesnake"	173
Alan Wells, "Fixing the Car"	174
Crystal Felix, "The Donut Man"	175
Kendra Wesley, "Fresh Delicious Bread"	176
Gina Abelkop, "Memory Stain"	177
Joseph Manglicmot, "Anger"	177
Carlos Mason, "Thirty Foot Waves"	178
Shyna Gianas, "Anything Else"	179
Marianne Samonte, "Diving into a Poem"	179

> A patron of the arts "makes himself the equal to the artist: he is building art into the world; he creates."
> – *Ezra Pound, 1915, in a letter to philanthropist John Quinn*

Dedication

Town of Love / Christian Lorenzo / Grade 4 / Central Elementary

This book is dedicated to the city and county school administrators and trustees of San Diego, who have supported student creativity by putting Border Voices poets into the classroom. A partial list of those deserving thanks would include Sue Braun, City Schools board member, who has been enthusiastic in her support of the project; City Schools Superintendent Alan Bersin and Dr. Anthony Alvarado, chancellor of the City Schools' Institute for Learning, as well as Staci Monreal, director of literacy for the Institute; Dr. Rudy M. Castruita, county superintendent of schools; Dr. Ellen Curtin of the National School District, and Barbara Schuch, head of the City Schools' Gifted and Talented program. Thanks also to Chris Dickerson, GATE resource teacher, and the many others who have made this program possible, with a special thanks to Dr. Dave Hermanson, now retired, who helped formulate the ideas on which the program is based.

> " I know, at last, that it is important to become an educated man. I thank you for that."
> – *A Hoover High School student, after a visit by a Border Voices poet-teacher*

Introduction: The Many Faces of Joy

Black Torch of Hell / George Le / Grade 8 / Mann Middle

July 23, 1999 was a hot, sweaty day to be stuck in traffic on I-5. Cars were backed up headed south, I was 15 minutes late getting to my office at the *Union-Tribune*, and the stack of articles I had to edit that evening was getting taller even as the gentleman in the shiny gray Volvo behind me decided that 3:30 p.m. on a BLISTERING day was a good time to test his new horn. Ooooh-WAAA! Oooh-WAAAA!

I smiled in my rear-view mirror. The beetle-browned businessman in the Volvo looked startled, but I didn't care. I was deliriously happy, even as my bright new sports coat wilted around my shoulders.

Here are the things I had to be grateful for:

1. We had just received word that the Border Voices Project, which I direct, would receive an $11,000 grant from the San Diego Commission for Arts and Culture for next year's poetry fair. The money would hardly cover the full cost of the fair and related events – the fee for Maya Angelou, who would appear at a pre-fair

warmup concert March 17, is a whopping $25,000 – but it was an essential part of the financial package we were putting together to get poetry into the schools and the community.

    2. The previous day, I'd received a phone call from a 13-year-old student, Jenny Garstang, that had revived my faith in the way poetry could transform lives, both for kids who participate in Border Voices poetry workshops, and for their families.

    3. One of my own poems had been selected for publication in a prestigious literary magazine devoted to the best sonnets of 1999.

    4. I had just spent an hour talking about poetry to a group of 50 senior citizens at MiraCosta College in Oceanside, and they had written a few good lines of poetry during that hour.

Morning Glory / Kelly Thornton
Grade 7 / Mesa Verde Middle

    It may seem odd, but each of these things, at that moment, was of equal value to me, because each was intimately intertwined. When a man or woman has spent years learning to write well – and teaching others to write – they finally come to realize that there is more to the art than the possibility of fame and an infrequent paycheck. If they are lucky, they first discover that writing poetry (or fiction or screenplays) is a personal and artistic exploration, a passageway to spiritual and emotional growth. And if they are VERY lucky, they learn something more – that writing is a social act, an endeavor to "purify the language of the tribe," and in the process to bring us word "of joy in widest commonalty spread" (Wordsworth).

    That was one reason I had gone up to MiraCosta College on that terribly hot day. I had been asked by a poet named Gordon Archibald to address his Life group of creative senior citizens, and I had not been sure I wanted to go. I was exhausted from crafting poems, from occasional teaching in the schools, and from administering the Border Voices Project in those spare hours when I was not earning my paycheck as an editor at the *Union-Tribune*. The last thing I wanted to do, as I dragged myself from bed that morning, was to go talk for an hour, and it was only a sense of duty – a grudging recognition of the societal responsibilities of a poet – that got me on the freeway headed north. I'm afraid I was a bit disconsolate as I walked into that stifling, jam-packed classroom at MiraCosta.

But then I saw the faces.

There were men who seem blighted by age, thin gray and trembling, but with bright and eager eyes. There were dark-haired women who could have been 40, smiling with anticipation. They listened as I recited Yeats and Janet Lewis, my own poems and those by Border Voices students, and then – after I had given them some brief instructions – they picked up their pens and began writing. They wrote about what it was like to wake up in a hospital bed after a stroke, and how they surprised themselves with their dispassion, with their sense that their nurses and doctors and wives were incredibly far away. They wrote of their children, and their children's children, of their hope that their one true love was still waiting for them, somewhere.

They wrote poetry. And afterwards, they came up with their newly minted poems and asked me to edit them, and one short gray woman with an incredible smile asked me to come again because "we have so much to learn."

It is moments like these that make all the hard work of the Border Voices Poetry Project worthwhile. Although I cannot go to every school and every class that the Border Voices poets teach in every year – around 200 schools have hired our poets over the last six years – I hear stories, and I catch, at odd intervals, frissons of joy.

Here is one instance of that:

April 19, 1999

We all had trouble waking up that Sunday. The night before, the second day of the annual Poetry Fair had ended with a big party at the Point Loma home of a Border Voices volunteer. I had vague memories of Irish poet Eavan Boland on the floor in the den, being led through New Age exercises by a marketing woman from the *Union-Tribune*; and then there was Mexico City poet Alberto Blanco, surrounded by a crowd of admirers, all of them entranced by his wise humility, his soft-spoken brilliance.

Shards and fragments of memory wavered around me as I picked up the newspaper. I opened to the local section – and immediately stopped, entranced. There was a long story about the Poetry Fair, but that wasn't what held me, I'd been expecting it. What surprised me was a picture of a young girl writing on a blackboard we'd had at the fair, and this is what she wrote:

If I die, shall I die in Spring?
Amidst the flowers, and birds singing my name,
And the sweet smell of life
When everything is alive?
Nay, I cannot die in Spring.

She had signed the poem "Jenny Garstang," and I immediately began a debate with myself, a debate that continued over a glass of wine that evening with a friend.

"She couldn't have written that poem. Look at the cadences, the wisdom. The poem is both a song of joy about life and a cry against death, and it is imbued with a sense that both joy and death are intertwined and equally inevitable. Besides, look at that old-fashioned, 19th-century language. It has to be a poem by a lesser-known poet from Victorian England."

The poem nagged at me. So eventually I wrote Jenny's mother, Marlene, who promised that her daughter would write me. Here is what Jenny, who is 13, told me:

"I am Jenny Garstang... The reason I am writing is that I feel I can give you the best answer to your question of who wrote the poem on the board. The author of that poem is me. I am honored that you enjoyed my poem so much, and I wanted to send you the rest:"

When Shall I Die

If I die, shall I die in Spring?
Amidst the flowers, and birds singing my name,
And the sweet smell of life
When everything is alive?
Nay, I cannot die in Spring.

Then shall I die in Summer?
The hot lazy days of sitting in the shade of the willow,
Watching the clouds drift by.
Or swimming in the cool waters of a lake.
Shall I lay in the shade and close my eyes forever?
Nay, I cannot die in Summer.

And what of Autumn?
When the leaves turn golden and red,

And swirl and dance in the breeze.
Will I then sleep forever,
In this chaotic paradise?
Nay, I cannot die in Autumn.

Then shall I die in Winter?
As the white, lacy snow falls.
And the lakes freeze and the ground becomes white.
When all is still, and all is asleep,
as the embers glow in the fire,
Will I lay down and sleep, too, and never awaken for Spring?
Nay, I cannot die in Winter.

Life After Death / Jonathan Meas
Grade 8 / Mann Middle

Then when shall I die?
In those few seconds between seasons,
When time stops . . .
and waits, as if holding its breath.
Will I then stop as well?
Nay! For as long as I live, I will live forever!

    In her letter, Jenny went on to say that she wrote the poem at the Border Voices Fair. "I was so inspired by all of the famous poets that I simply had to write. Unfortunately, the original copy of this poem was lost except for the first verse, which was caught in the picture. I have since rewritten the poem, keeping the same basic idea in mind. The last line was part of the original poem, too."
    I immediately called Jenny to congratulate her on her poem, to learn a little about her background – and to give her, without her knowledge, a little test.
    It had seemed to me that the first stanza of her poem was incredibly strong, that the subsequent stanzas were of a high caliber (though perhaps not as breathtaking as those first five lines), but that the poem fell off at the end. All of the subdued bravery of the first four stanzas was still present at the beginning of the last stanza, with its lovely lines:

Then when shall I die?
In those few seconds between seasons,
When time stops . . .
And waits, as if holding its breath.

But then the poem erupts, as if the vision of death was too hard to take – it erupts in what seems at first sight a totally unbelievable statement:

Will I then stop as well?
Nay! For as long as I live, I will live forever!

When I pointed this out to Jenny – with the suggestion that perhaps those last lines should be cut or rephrased – she was absolutely adamant that they were right the way they were, though she acknowledged that she didn't fully understand them.

I then suggested that she try her hand at some alternate versions of the lines, and she promised she would.

I was doubly impressed. Jenny had passed both parts of my test: she had displayed a sureness about her poem, even the weakest part of it, that showed an artistic instinct for what was emotionally right; at the same time, she was willing to consider rewriting those parts of it which (while emotionally right) still might need some work.

I hinted to Jenny that what was needed was a few lines of explanation, of grounding, that might make that last line less unbelievable. Something like:

Nay! For as long as I live, I will live
each moment, each season,
as if Autumn's chaos were forever,
as if Spring's sweet smell were forever,
For as long as I live, I will live forever.

But I am sure Jenny's final version will be much better than mine. It's her poem, after all.

And it was her joy that I caught as listened to her reminisce about her earliest writing (she crafted song lyrics at age 7), her dad's efforts to write a novel, and her gratitude to Border Voices poet Veronica Cunningham, who taught her, through drawing and music, that "art doesn't have to be realistic, perfect. Until I took a class with Veronica, I thought everything had to be scientific and perfect, and I was so frustrated, because nothing is perfect."

Jenny's mother, Marlene, is a fan of her daughter: "There's wisdom in her poetry, and in the music she composes. Sometimes it surprises me." What is just as surprising and wonderful is how Jenny, in the first stanza of her poem, has written five good lines of poetry. And as Ezra Pound says, if someone writes six good lines of poetry, they're immortal. Jenny, at 13, is almost there.

Faces. Old and young, smooth or lined: all of them so full of joy.

Perhaps Wordsworth was right. Perhaps, in capturing our lives in the rhythms of poetry, we inhabit our own experience more fully, and share it more fully with others. Our lives become like a book, the most fascinating of books, always changing and always full of surprises – and we learn to respect others that way, in their endless variety and possibilities.

In the following pages you will find bits and pieces of lives, poems by major poets as well as students, and I hope you will discover them to be as delightful and full of possibility as I do.

Jack Webb, Director
Border Voices Poetry Project

Eating Lizard / Jonathan Vance / Grade 4 / Canyon View Elementary

Within Our Reach / Cristy Rodriguez / Grade 8 / Bonita Vista Middle

Acknowledgements

This book and the April 2000 Poetry Fair are the result of a collaboration between dozens of poets, teachers and organizations; special thanks go to those organizations and individuals who helped underwrite this book and the Fair. Among those who contributed were the James S. Copley Foundation; the John R. and Jane F. Adams Endowment; Deborah Szekely, president of the Eureka Communities foundation; the California Arts Council; the Fieldstone Foundation; Shelle and Gabriel Wisdom, and the San Diego Commission for Arts and Culture. A special debt is owed the coterie of volunteer administrators who kept everything running smoothly through hard work leavened with humor: Chris Dickerson, Chris Baron, Sylvia Levinson, and Celia Sigmon. Thanks also to the judges who selected the student art and poetry for this anthology, including Matthew Costello, Trissy McGhee, Melissa Marconi, Hector Martinez, Cali Linfor, Chris Fell and Sabrina Youmans, as well as to the three internationally acclaimed poets who selected student poems for awards: Pulitzer Prize winner Mark Strand, Billy Collins and Genny Lim. And a VERY special thanks to *The San Diego Union-Tribune* for agreeing to co-sponsor the project, and to publish student poems, fiction and essays in the newspaper at the time of the fair.

Following is a list of others who have contributed money, in-kind contributions, or moral support to the Border Voices Poetry Project:

The Administrators Association of San Diego City Schools; David Antin; Claudia Axel; Barnes & Noble/Bookstar; Vincent M. Blocker of San Diego State University; California Poets in the Schools; Brandon Cesmat; the San Diego Chargers; the San Diego County Office of Education, with special thanks to Dr.

Why Not? / Patricia Greliak / Grade 8 / Muirlands Middle

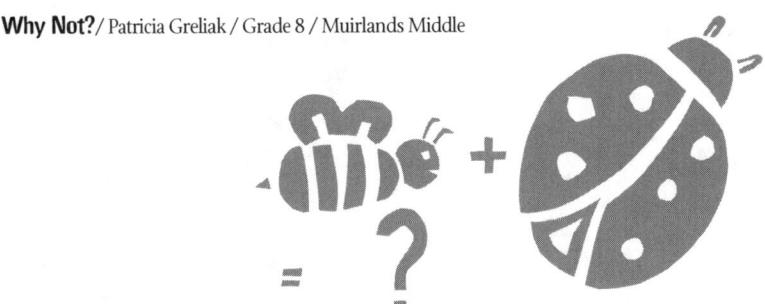

Acknowledgements

Rudy M. Castruita, superintendent; Rosalia Salinas, Director II, bilingual education; Silvia C. Dorta-Duque de Reyes; and Richard A. Harrison.

Thanks also to Beverly Cramb; Veronica Cunningham; Glover Davis of the Master of Fine Arts Program in Creative Writing at San Diego State University; Doug Dickerson; Glory Foster; Kermeen Fristrom; Steve Garber; Jana Gardner; César González-T., founding chair of Chicano Studies at Mesa College; the Greater San Diego Council of Teachers of English; Marian Haddad; minerva (Gail Hawkins); Georgette James; Leslie L.J. Reilly, the graphic artist who swiftly and efficiently designed this book, the fair poster, and other odds and ends, astonishing everyone (as usual) with her joyful brilliance in the face of constant deadlines; Tamara Johnson; Roxanne Young Kilbourne; Chuck Korkeegian; Steve Kowit of Southwestern College; Herb Klein, editor-in-chief of the Copley Newspapers; Hope Meek; Jim Milner; Joe Milosch; Regina Morin; Jill Moses; Johnnierenee Nia Nelson; Sally Owen; Leroy Quintana of Mesa College; *The Poetry Conspiracy* magazine; Michele Renneisen, community relations representative for the *Union-Tribune;* the San Diego Padres; the San Diego Unified School District, with special thanks to city school board member Sue Braun, Dave Hermanson, Barbara Schuch, and Ellie Dorman, and to the staff of the Institute for Learning, including Staci Monreal, director of literacy; *San Diego Writers' Monthly;* Drew Schlosberg, community relations manager for the *Union-Tribune;* Quincy Troupe of UCSD; Jerry Warren, former editor of the *Union-Tribune;* Pat Washington of SDSU; and Karin Winner, the current editor of the *Union-Tribune.*

The Fair was funded in part by a grant from the California Council for the Humanities, a state program of the National Endowment for the Humanities.

Major Poets
Poems & Biographies

Chaotic Love / Sheena Deguzman / Grade 10 / Morse High

Billy Collins

Tiptoeing gingerly past the chaotic artistic minefield of the 20th Century, Billy Collins has found a way to recapture a portion of the once-huge audience that poetry has lost to novels, films and video games. This is no small achievement after a period of nearly 100 years in which sales of poetry have fallen well below those of cookbooks, technical journals and religious tracts – an artistic defeat to which poets themselves have contributed by creating what has been described as a deliberately minor, unmelodious and "penitent art."

Balding and winsome, with crow's feet laughing around his eyes, Collins packs auditoriums with both students and greying baby boomers who eagerly sign his five books, praise him for writing "the funniest poems I ever heard," and commiserate with him for his battles with the University of Pittsburgh Press. The Press printed three of Collins' books, but now refuses to release the rights to Random House, which is trying to print a collection of selected poems as an honor due one of the country's best-selling writers.

While Collins' success is undeniable, the reasons for it can be difficult to see, obscured as they are by the gushing and unhelpful praise of his admirers. The novelist John Updike, for example, has written that Collins' poems "describe all the worlds that are and were and some others besides" – a description that would be applicable to the work of Shakespeare or Dante perhaps, and might cause the unwary to pick up Collins expecting to find everything from the fall of kingdoms to the loss of a loved one, the misery and joy that lies in marriage, the ecstasy of triumph, and the fear of death.

The reader will find nothing as grand and all-inclusive as that. Instead, he will find the poet shedding an ironic tear over the Three Blind Mice, or lying on his back watching the clouds and wondering what the weather was like before Eden. He will find, as in the accompanying poem, gentle narratives with a humorous twist, where the author envies and admires the "learned birds" who know whether the wild berries he covets are actually good to eat.

The careful and persistent reader may also find the secret to Collins' success, as well as some reasons to be concerned about his future as a writer. For Collins, a professor of Romantic poetry, has adopted the techniques of the great 18th and 19th Century poets he studies as an academic: he writes poems that are personal, emotional, agreeable and reflective, something like Wordsworth's "Tintern Abbey" but with a bit of humor. Like the late e.e. cummings and Robinson Jeffers, Collins has obtained celebrity by offering readers what they have been famished for – poems that are easy to read and melodious to the ear, and in that way totally unlike the deliberately "antipopular" verse of many latter-day poets. At the same time, Collins' poems – like those of cummings and Jeffers – wear an intriguing mask of modernity because of their hip quirkiness.

The danger is that Collins will follow cummings and Jeffers in being content with easy solutions, satisfied with insufficiently reflective verse, and eventually find himself subject to growing critical and popular reservations. Even now, early in his career, Collins seems a little too happy going for the specious joke, as when he alludes to Marianne Moore – that brave and formidable poet-critic who struck fear in such literary lions as Robert Lowell – as a "titmouse, fluttering about / in its own tiny sphere of excitement . . . "

Despite these early reservations, Collins is a bright and promising part of the modern literary landscape. A poet of wit in an age of confusion and anger, he has performed brilliantly on such showcases as NPR's "Fresh Air" and "A Prairie Home Companion"; delighted thousands of readers, and won numerous well-deserved awards.

Yellow Berries

I stop to look into the undergrowth
at the edge of a green playing field –
a tangle of bushes,
small yellow berries in clusters.

No scalpel is singing
across my abdomen this morning,

nor have I been tied to a chair
in order to be questioned, slapped,
and questioned again.

And this gives me the time
to stand here and wonder
whether these berries are safe to eat or not
if I were starving, say,
if there were no nearby market
where all kinds of berries
may be purchased in great quantities.

Three sparrows,
who probably know the answer,
surprise me when they twitter up from the knotted vines
and as I watch them fly off,

I decide that when the day comes,
I will refuse to die,
just chin-up-arms-folded refuse,
unless I am guaranteed clusters
of yellow berries
hanging in the afterlife,

a spacious green field,
and learned birds darting through the air.

– Billy Collins

© 1999 by Billy Collins. This poem is printed here for the first time.

Sharon Olds

Few modern poets arouse readers' enthusiasm as much as Sharon Olds, who explores sexuality, the family, and the injustices of today's world with sometimes graphic but always tender detail. She captured the attention of the literary world with her first book, *Satan Says*, and has gone on to win most of the major prizes, meanwhile teaching a new generation of poets as an acclaimed professor at New York University and elsewhere.

But she has always remained a deeply private person. The following is part of a rare interview, conducted a few years ago by the editor of this anthology. In this excerpt, Olds discusses poetry with a frankness that contains a few surprises, including a fresh approach to so-called free verse as well as her own lightly ironic opinions about the use of personal history in literary criticism:

QUESTION: In your early poems, you seemed to be wrestling primarily with personal demons – with the image of an alcoholic and dominating father figure, with the bewildered and sometimes cruel mother figure. In *The Dead and the Living*, your second book, there were poems that dealt with public horrors, such as the torture of innocents in police states. Some critics have suggested that this was an attempt to merge the two concerns, to show a relationship between domestic and public violence – a concern continued in your book *The Gold Cell*. Would you say that's an accurate assessment?

OLDS: In *The Dead and the Living* I happened to write a lot of poems about the outside world and a lot about the family, but I'm not trying to connect them. When I put a book together, I'm not trying to write across ideas. We write poems to write something that seems true, and that has its appropriate beauty and ugliness.

Q: How would you describe the techniques you use in your poetry? What are the principles of prosody which you follow?

OLDS: When I look at my own poems, I can see the quatrain of the hymnal behind all my work.

Q: That's fascinating. I've heard you described as one of our more powerful free-verse poets.

OLDS: I was trained in what Denise Levertov calls "reusable forms," such as sonnets and villanelles. But no one will ever see those early poems of mine. The old formal stuff was wonderful, but in my hands it didn't have sufficient strength. I couldn't sing with it.

Nevertheless, the poems that I have published to date have clearly been based on quatrains. This is the formal or dead grid on which the hopefully living structure of my poetry can dance. If you scan it, you'll find the typical variations of feet, the trochees and iambs.

Q: I've noticed there's very little biographical information available on you. Your publisher didn't have any information, and there's very little in magazines or on your dust jackets.

OLDS: I don't give out biographical information. It seems to me that the important thing about a poet is his or her poems, not their lives. The biography of the poet doesn't interest me inside or outside.

Q: And yet there are things about T.S. Eliot's life, for example, that help us understand how he wrote "The Waste Land."

OLDS: Did you know that Eliot wore green eye shade to make himself look more sensitive?

Q: You're pulling my leg, aren't you?

OLDS: No, no – I read it in a biography, so it has to be true.

Sharon Olds' most recent book is *Blood, Tin, Straw* (Alfred A. Knopf, 1999).

The Prepositions

When I started Junior High, I thought
I'd probably be a Behavior Problem
all my life, John Muir Grammar
the spawning grounds, the bad-seed bed,
   but
the first morning at Willard, the dawn
of seventh grade, they handed me a list
of forty-five prepositions, to learn
by heart. I stood in the central court
   yard,
enclosed garden that grew cement,
my pupils followed the line of the arches
up and over, up and over, like
alpha waves, *about, above,*
across, along, among, around, an
odd comfort began, in me,
before, behind, below, beneath,
beside, between, I stood in that sand
   stone
square, and started to tame. *Down,*
from, in, into, near, I was
located there, watching the Moorish half-
circles rise and fall. *Off,*
on, onto, out, outside, we
came from sixth grades all over the city
to meet each other for the first time,
White tennis-club boys who did not
speak to me, White dorks
who did, Black student-council guys
   who'd gaze
off, above my head, and the Black
plump goof-off, who walked past and
suddenly flicked my sweater-front, I
   thought to shame me.
Over, past, since, through,
that was the year my father came home
   in the
middle of the night with those thick
   earthworms
of blood on his face, trilobites of
elegant gore, cornice and crisp
waist of the extinct form,
till, to, toward, under, the
lining of my uterus convoluted,
shapely and scarlet as the jointed leeches
of wound clinging to my father's face in
   that
mask, *unlike, until, up,* I'd
walk, day and night, into
the Eden of the list, *hortus enclosus*
   where
everything had a place. I was *in*
relation to, upon, with, and when I
got to forty-five I could start over,
pull the hood of the list down over
my brain again. It was the first rest
I had had from my mind. My glance
   would run
slowly along the calm electro-
cardiogram of adobe cloister,
within, without, I'd repeat the prayer I'd
received, a place in the universe,
meaningless but a place, an exact
   location –
Telegraph, Woolsey, Colby, Russell –
Berkeley, 1956,
fourteen, the breaking of childhood,
   beginning of memory.

– Sharon Olds

Reprinted by permission of the author. From the book *Blood, Tin, Straw* © 1999, Alfred A. Knopf, Inc.

Martín Espada

The first-time reader can be forgiven for opening Martín Espada's books with trembling and uncertain fingers. He will have heard, perhaps, that Espada is a propagandist for the poor, a scourge of the establishment (especially the U.S. establishment), and a bitter enemy of "writers of color" who have "peeled off their skin in a striptease for white politicians" – that Espada is, in other words, a political poet of the most virulent stripe. And political poets have gotten rather a bad name in the last few decades. In a passage that drips with genteel sarcasm, Paul Fussell describes the uninspired formula for much modern political verse:

> "(such poems) deploy vaguely surrealistic images in unmetered colloquial idiom to urge acceptable opinions: that sex is a fine thing . . . that corporations are corrupt . . . and that women get a dirty deal. All very true and welcome. Yet what is lamentably missing is the art that makes poems re-readable once we have fathomed what they say."

The literary magazines are uniformly enthusiastic about Espada, calling him "the true poet laureate of this nation," but that's of little help to our uncertain reader. As Robert Bly has noted, "Although more bad poetry is being published than ever before in American history, most of the reviews are positive . . . mediocre poetry (is) praised, or never attacked" by literary journals that exist not to provide a disinterested perspective on new books, but to publicize them.

To our hypothetically fearful reader, I can only say: read Espada. There is much in his books that will disturb them, and there are also long passages of angry poetry that seem to have been written merely to illustrate Fussell's tongue-in-cheek comment. But there are also brilliant and humorous poems – such as the one on the facing page – that paint a much-needed portrait of those who are poor and ignored, or whose miseries are accentuated by the whims of a sometimes-savage officialdom. At his best, Espada gives the lie to those undereducated modern-day critics who claim that politics has no place in poetry. Such critics forget that political/satiric poetry has a long and exciting history, starting with Aristophanes and Juvenal, through the angry Milton of "On the Last Massacre in Piemont," to (in recent years) Lorca, Philip Levine, Ernesto Cardenal and Pablo Neruda. If Espada continues to develop, attuning his ear to the rhythms of anger so powerfully explored by his brilliant predecessors, he may eventually take his place in the Pantheon of satire.

The question, of course, is whether Espada will continue to develop, or if he will be misled by his admirers and remain content with the sometimes flat verse which they applaud. If so, he may end up joining the list of those lamented by the great Polish political poet Zbigniew Herbert, who noted that many of his fellow writers had thrown out traditional technique because they felt it was more important to "battle with tyranny and lies." The poets became journalists, obsessed with "the black foam of newspapers," and as a result their poems did not age well: they had lost the secret "of enchanting words into form resistant to time / without which there is no phrase worth remembering / and words are like sand."

Martín Espada is a former tenant lawyer who is the author of six books of poetry, the most recent being *A Mayan Astronomer in Hell's Kitchen* (W.W. Norton, 2000). He has won numerous awards, including a 1998 Pushcart Prize and the 1999 Independent Publisher Book Award. He is an associate professor at the University of Massachusetts-Amherst.

For the Jim Crow Mexican Restaurant in Cambridge, Massachusetts Where My Cousin Esteban Was Forbidden to Wait Tables Because He Wears Dreadlocks

I have noticed that the hostess in peasant dress,
the wait staff and the boss
share the complexion of a flour tortilla.
I have spooked the servers at my table
by trilling the word *burrito*.
I am aware of your T-shirt solidarity
with the refugees of the Américas
since they steam in your kitchen.
I know my cousin Esteban the sculptor
rolled tortillas in your kitchen with the fingertips
of ancestral Puerto Rican cigarmakers.
I understand he wanted to be a waiter,
but you proclaimed his black dreadlocks unclean,
so he hissed in Spanish
and his apron collapsed on the floor.

May La Migra handcuff the wait staff
as suspected illegal aliens from Canada;
may a hundred mice dive from the oven
like diminutive leaping dolphins
during your Board of Health inspection;
may the kitchen workers strike, sitting
with folded hands as enchiladas blacken
and twisters of smoke panic the customers;
may a Zapatista squadron commandeer the refrigerator,
liberating a pillar of tortillas at gunpoint;
may you hallucinate dreadlocks
braided in thick vines around your ankles;
and may the Aztec gods pinned like butterflies
to the menu wait for you in the parking lot
at midnight, demanding that you spell their names.

– Martín Espada

© 2000 by Martín Espada. Reprinted by permission of the author. This poem also will appear in the book *A Mayan Astronomer in Hell's Kitchen*, W.W. Norton & Company, to be published in April 2000.

Mark Strand is the former Poet Laureate of the United States, a Pulitzer Prize winner – and something of a puzzle to his admirers, who heap him with awards while disagreeing violently about what he has to say. For those new to Strand's work, we can begin illustrating the problem by quoting from one of his most popular and anthologized poems, "Eating Poetry":

Mark Strand

Ink runs from the corners of my mouth.
There is no happiness like mine
I have been eating poetry . . .

The poems are gone.
The light is dim.
The dogs are on the basement stairs and coming up . . .

The poor librarian begins to stamp her feet and weep.
She does not understand.
When I get on my knees and lick her hand,
she screams.

I am a new man,
I snarl at her and bark.
I romp with joy in the bookish dark.

It is poems like these that caused the literary historian David Perkins, a usually discerning observer, to describe Strand as a surrealist. But as *The Norton Anthology of Modern Poetry* has pointed out, Strand's poems are not really surrealist – the language is clear and simple, with none of the terribly disjunctive adjectives of the surrealists, no "hungry fanged roses mating in the mailed garden." What we find instead are powerful expressions of complex feelings through the vehicle of astonishingly original extended metaphors. These metaphors create a dreamlike quality, but have none of the imprecision of surrealism. In "Eating Poetry," Strand is using an extended metaphor to describe what it feels like to give himself up to a great poet, to imbue himself with the rhythms and the world view of a Yeats or a Rilke – to "romp with joy in the bookish dark." In other poems both early and late, Strand continues the search for transformation, a search that frequently enters the realm of nightmare as Strand's poetic persona or the characters he describes find themselves resting in soundless rooms where "nothing curled in the air / but the sound of nothing, / the hymn of nothing . . ."

The critic David Kirby has described Strand as seeking "self-effacement" through his poetry, but – as the preceding discussion indicates – it may be more accurate to describe him as a man in search of a skin that fits in these often difficult times. The cooly distraught Strand persona, as found in his poems, frequently reminds me of the pebbles in the Zbigniew Herbert poem: "to the end they will look at us / with a calm and very clear eye." When I picture Strand's poetic persona as a conscious stone, with "its ardour and coldness / . . . just and full of dignity," I seem to see him more accurately; and when I imagine that rock shivering with a trace of anxiety, opening an eye as I hold it in the heat of my hand, I seem to see that persona with the greatest clarity.

In his most recent book, *Blizzard of One*, Strand appears to confront that searching and troubled persona more directly than ever, and to hint at answers – for example, in the poem "Old Man Leaves Party." The character in this poem goes into the woods and strips naked, thinking "how could I not / Be only myself, this dream of flesh, from moment to moment?" Calmer and more accepting, with a meditative mood reminiscent of the great Romantics, Strand's latest poems seem to say that he has found a new skin, and a home that both we and he can delight in.

Lake

To drowse away the summer on a lake
*
To feel the limitations of the lake
*
To count the lake's two colors
*
To feel that something is wrong with the lake
*
I really like the lake, said the woman next door
*
You push a lake out of the way, but it comes right back
*
A lake could mean the end of chaos
*
A lake swallows itself every night
*
I like this lake, too, I said to the woman next door
*
There once was a lake with only one wave
*
Fifty young men were staring into the lake
*
If you speak to the lake, you must ask yourself why
*
To test the true material of the lake
*
To dip the oars of sleep into the surface of the lake

To feel the lake give birth to words for itself
*
A lake could fall into the wrong hands
*
Even an artificial lake needs real water
*
Oh the lake is beautiful, and meaningless, and I love it
*
What lake is that you're talking about
*
No lake at all – I'm bad at remembering lakes
*
Is it the way a lake looks or how it feels that matters
*
In that respect a lake is like a chair
*
The lake was full of stars, the moon, the tops of trees
*
Someone was playing a trombone across the lake
*
On this side of the lake a silence was building up

– Mark Strand

© 2000 by Mark Strand. This poem is printed here for the first time.

It must be fun, sometimes, to be Genny Lim. After publishing two exquisite and powerful plays in 1989 and 1991, and a promising collection of poetry (*Winter Place*, 1989), the San Francisco poet turned to performance poetry and the crafting of improvisatory works on-stage, backed by jazz musicians.

"There's something exciting about watching something occurring spontaneously in an improvisatory way," Lim said in a 1996 interview.

Genny Lim

"Cause you feel like you're part of history at that moment. It's not happening at any other place or time, and it's not happening in the past and it won't happen in the future."

Lim has won applause and awards for her performances, which rely on "the power of voice and demeanor (so that) another transmission occurs that you cannot negate or underestimate." In 1996, she was featured on PBS' "United States of Poetry."

One of the problems with performance poetry, of course, is that it is not as compelling when transferred from the stage to the page. Without the backing of musicians, the "call and response" of living voice and jazz riffs, an improvisatory poem can seem incomplete, as in the example on the adjoining page. But one must respect Lim's decision to de-emphasize crafted poetry and prose in favor of a musical-verbal hybrid, even if some of her fans have a continuing nostalgia for such marvelous early achievements as the play *Paper Angels*, from which the following excerpt is taken:

The setting is the Angel Island Detention Center in San Francisco in 1915. The central character, Chin Moo, had spent 40 years alone in China, waiting for her husband to return from the United States. When he finally came for her, he was an old man with "chicken skin and crane hair." But she agreed to return with him to America.

After their voyage to the United States, Chin Moo and her husband are detained at Angel Island for weeks. Immigration officials finally tell the man he cannot enter the country because he has a liver disease, although Chin Moo is welcome. Alone in the men's section of the center, the husband hangs himself.

Now Chin Moo is sitting in the detention center, fingering her red wedding tunic and mourning her husband:

CHIN MOO: You were so handsome on our wedding day! I was so proud to be your wife. You told me I was as pretty as a plum blossom and you could hardly wait to pluck me off the branch. (*laughs*) Imagine me, dressed up in bright, fancy clothes and funny hats. Walking down gold-paved streets with my hand tucked in your elbow. (*pausing sadly*) Why did you come back for me? Why didn't you marry an American girl and forget me? Don't you know I had buried you a long time ago? I can't even remember what I looked like. (*touches her face*) A dream is good only when you have someone to share it with.

As entertaining and provocative as Lim's performance poetry can be – and at times it can be very entertaining – one can be forgiven for regretting the months and years Lim has <u>not</u> spent crafting those moments that will last beyond her lifetime, and ours.

A Hip Invention

Trying to find satori in the '90s was
like driving blind
You had the wheel but you
didn't know where you were going

Love is a hip invention
A twenty first century novelty
There is no common language among
    birds, men or trees
No dharma among thieves or postmod
    ern sutras
Computer mantras come in innovative
    software and
human emotions are stimulated by profit
Out here, the seven hills overlooking the
    Bay rise
like seven gaudy Buddhas
Once lapis lazuli, the sea is sewage

There is no nuclear path to enlighten
    ment
without sacrificial death
No cross between obsidian and light
    without pain

Native peoples worshipped the Eagle
    who flew
into the sun to bring us back the light
we are the sun which brings the light
We think we are the drum which beats
    the world alive
We think we are the world which nature
    must survive
But the millennium drones with the
    expulsions of
missiles, tanks and uzis
as we recite out children's names
Hiroshima, Bay of Pigs, El Salvador,
    Persian Gulf . . .
Fingering our memories like rosaries

O holy trinity of technocracy!
E pluribus unum
Capital, profit and consumption

I want to stop time and
twist it open till it cries
I want to explode time and
twist it open till it cries
I want to explode time because it's stuck
    and
I am stuck in it
I am stuck and you are stuck
We are stuck and
our children are stuck
in needles and veins

We are stuck
inside the barrel of a gun
inside a whiskey bottle and piss
inside pregnant bellies and perfume
inside the graffiti
inside sex
inside the ozone
inside monkey talk and think tanks
inside white skin
inside self-hate
inside death
inside money
inside shit
inside a condom of reality
inside a dysfunctional family
inside our bodies
inside our being
inside ourselves
inside this White House of
America

Love was a hip invention
before language

– Genny Lim

© 2000 by Genny Lim. This poem is published here for the first time.

Looking Into The Future / Tsubasa Yamaguchi / Grade 8 / Standley Middle

Empty

The wind blew through me
like black knotted fish bones
beneath an oil lamp.
The raven's orange moon
choking on its own white feathers
failed to catch me
and I lost myself.
The rain tasted like moss
and soap.
Why doesn't anyone tell me these things?
How could I see that
cloudless indigo banana leaves
taste sweeter under the cold north star?
The twenty rows of mango trees
strain and wheeze, unable to explain
that in the clouds the snow sees its soul,
that, on the wall, the top hat I'd forgotten
is hanging itself.
I see too late
the octopus of time
knotting its arms outside the window.

Sarah Lambert
Grade 11, La Jolla High
Poet-Teacher: Jill Moses
Teacher: Robin Visconti

The Burned Doll

One eye shut more
than the other
missing fingers
missing toes
burned-up face
burned-up everywhere
Eyes not sparkling
hair not shiny
dress full of ash
shoes full of holes
My grandma gave
me this burned doll
to show me that you don't
always have to spend
money to get something
beautiful

Jessica Trail
Grade 9, Chula Vista High
Poet-Teacher: Jim Milner
Teacher: Jonathan Barnes

"A Face With Heart"
Tina Utter/Grade 8/Standley Middle

Nocturnal City

I can hear the city
  like a dog barking,
      talking
      talking
      talking.
The chip of people's shoes
  walking down the sidewalk,
      sirens
  people calling taxis
      taxi
      taxi.
The stores filled with shoppers
      working
      eating
      working
      eating.
Kids running down a long street.
The lights flickering
      on
      off
  calling me,
  calling my name.
The city moves heavy
    like a sleepless elephant
    crashing through the night.
The streets keep moving,
  a long wave of light.
It slithers like a snake,
  never stopping.
It's full of explosions
      laughter,
  calling me again
      into the night.

Julian Goodin
Grade 5, Cadman Elementary
Poet-Teacher: Celia Sigmon
Teacher: Jean Feinstein

Gridlock Games

Enjoy the ride from point A to point B.
Can we go buy a translucent blue cement mixer?
A cement mixer is a functional and ingenious alternative to a refrigerator.
A bipartisan effort to utilize nose hairs has been denied
in a bubbling rage by common time-fillers.

3.8 percent of men who admitted to applying make-up in the car
made their debut in the rush-hour twilight.

Can animal lovers and four million anonymous users be wrong
about space-age toilet paper from homegrown imports?
The cargo side-doors first appeared on American soil.
Hoods up to all commuters in the Metropolitan area.
The cement mixer has once again collapsed under the immense
   weight of the traffic!
What can we do?
Translucent blue cement mixers are all the rage
in the Metropolitan area.

      Devon Galindo
      Grade 6, San Pasqual Union
      Poet-Teacher: Brandon Cesmat
      Teacher: Ken Beeunas

"A Tale of Two Cities"
Nicole Ellis/Grade 7/Mesa Verde Middle

A Simple Crystal Memory

In my left hand, I hold a piece of crystal.
Black, hard, almost obsidian.
Cold, dry, masterfully carved black crystal
shaped like a small elephant.
The excellent craftsmanship and the rarity of the crystal
makes it valuable.
The memories it holds of my ancestors
makes it priceless.

The crystal is a remnant
of my great-granddad's crystal store
in the simple paradise of China,
before it was taken by the king's troops
to fund the war.
My great-granddad was forced to move
to the countryside.

My granddad gave it to me years ago.
Always cautious, he did not wait until it was too late.
Thanks to celestial generosity,
he is still laughing and grieving.
This elephant is the fountain of my youth,
the fountain of my memories.

Zhengkan Wang
Grade 8, Murilands Middle
Poet-Teacher: Glory Foster
Teacher: Wayne Bardos

"Solar Vortex"
Peter Lai/Grade 7/Mesa Verde Middle

My Mother's Ring

opals
my birthstone, by some coincidence
standing in the pawn shop the day you bought it
your long hair down your back
dreams not yet annihilated
by children you really didn't want and the life you settled for
six of them dancing in a circle
me as a small child
gazing into your jewelry box
sparsely furnished because
you were never one for luxuries
"you can have this when you turn thirteen"
and I wanted it
not because it fit on my finger--it didn't
only because little girls like pretty things
to hide away and admire occasionally
thirteen came and went
though it seemed as far away as the distance to China
and I still wanted it
something beautiful to contrast my awkward self
"when you're older"
fifteen came, with the sprouting of resentment
I still desired the ring,
for it hadn't been offered
like you promised
sixteen
even if I had recalled, silent still
because we never spoke
for fear of fighting over trivial things
that concealed deeper meaning
last July
in a blue velvet box
on my desk
like the ocean or the intense sky just after dusk
I put it on
a perfect size for an imperfect hand
glad to be finally worthy of the present
to know you hadn't forgotten
"don't lose this" you said
and I never will
a solid form of gold and stone
a link between us

Carolyn Pratt
Grade 11, La Jolla High
Poet-Teacher: Jill Moses
Teacher: Robin Visconti

Work

It is the city
        With businessmen bustling to
Work, and thinking of their wives and children,
And the shuffling of papers and the slurping of coffee.
There is traffic and the curious ring of a phone and
Work of the chopping and dicing of the cats' meat by mens' knives.
There are high, monstrous buildings with their little eyes and lights
And there are no trees.
There is the clanging of glasses and silverware in the
Restaurants while they get ready for the breakfast rush.
And there is the flicker of the bright, golden streetlights
Fading away in the early morning as the crimson red sun lurches
Over the monster skyscrapers.
There is the work of the taxi drivers
Starting their small yellow cars and their meters.
But there is a park, peacefully silent in the red, early-morning sun.
The gray benches are sadly empty and the pigeons with
Their brown jackets, snooze upon the large blue-gray statue
Of a famous man.
The still, large blue pond with its water fountain shining
Bright in the early morning
Sunlight, while a small coracle
Sits on its shore waiting, like a dog, waiting to be unleashed.

                        And there is work.

Spencer Reynolds
Grade 7, Standley Middle
Poet-Teacher: Tamara Johnson
Teacher: Patricia Barton

"Out of the Same Mold"
Bridget Lao/Grade 12/Morse High

The Power of My Culture

I come from long hours of tough
Labor in fields and making cars.
I come from eyes of passionate blue, brown and gold.
I come from Belgian cookies
And kooka-bread.
I come from humid days and
Storms that could blow your house down.
I come from tall people with gorgeous hair of chocolate brown.
I come from long days when the sun never sets.
I come from athletes, my parents, the greatest of all.
I come from two worlds that, somehow, molded into one.

Kassy Lee
Grade 4, Franklin
Poet-Teacher: Veronica Cunningham
Teacher: Sara Ellis

I'm a Fire-Breathing Dragon

I am as hot as a comet.
I am as large as a mansion.
Don't come close.
I might just bite.
Can't you see I am as big as can be?
I can burn as torrid as the sun
like a fire peeling off your skin--
Sizzle sizzle burn.
I glide over valleys, swiftly
over seas. Catch me if you can.
I am faster than a cheetah.
I am as dirty as a pig.
I am a fire-breathing dragon.
I can burn like acid. My fire
is a comet rushing to earth.

Alyssia Veiga
Grade 4, El Toyon Elementary
Poet-Teacher: Jill Moses
Teacher: Myrna Kahle

Sonic Boom"
Rowell Dela Cruz/Grade 10/Morse High

Dragon Boy

I pick up the plate,
stroking the smooth, round edges,
the cold porcelain biting my fingers.
I grip the precious heirloom tightly,
taking care not to let it slip,
and go crashing to the floor.
I gaze at the glossy surface,
studying every detail
of the shimmering piece of art.
The blue lace pattern dances
around the rim of the silver mist
from the mountains of China.
In the center of the plate,
a boy and a dragon dance,
fluidly, ceaselessly, trapped in time.
Staring at the shinning surface,
I see a reflection,
but it is not my own face.
It is the image of my grandfather,
and his father, and all of my ancestors
of long, long ago, living in a forgotten past.
The reflections seem to stretch into infinity,
each slightly dissimilar to the previous,
but all are linked through common traits.
The images merge together,
forming a single reflection,
and I find myself staring at my own face,
knowing that when the time comes,
I will join my ancestors,
living in the memories of future generations.
But for now, I am the boy
dancing around with the dragon.

Rob Low
Grade 8, Muirlands Middle
Poet-Teacher: Glory Foster
Teacher: Wayne Bardos

A Window on Logan

I wonder where
the flesh and curves of my
mother's, mother's, mother's body
vanished and disappeared to.
The years pass like sand
falling through her fingers,
the fine particles carried away
on the gust of a March breeze.
Delicious memories,
irresistible aromas, untouchable recipes,
enticing men strolling by in white suits,
snake-skin belts and black shiny shoes,
hats tilted sideways, their life going all ways
except the way they hoped it would.
These men swore they smelled Louisiana
seeping under the crack and through
the tiny holes of her iron-screen door, well-equipped
with locks and latches in LOGAN, where the bravest
great-grandmothers live alone picking collard and mustard
greens from their own backyards, never forgetting
to check for the snails. I sometimes miss
her kitchen, an appetite emergency room
that caused your mouth to water, taste buds to work overtime.
I watch Miss Walker, great-grandmother, reach out
with trembling hands to turn off the stove.
But with 80 years of experience,
her hands still stir and serve black-eyed peas,
greens, ham hocks, and hot-water corn bread
until finally wiping her forehead with the back
of her translucent hand, wearing her veins proudly
like bracelets, red, blue, and violet bangles around her wrists,
bones peeking through, obviously wrinkled and cracked,
she kept no secrets.

Finally her body, unable to keep up, passes away,
life still pumping through her heart,
fingers clutching a fork even though she'll soon let go.
And with swollen knuckles and a crooked finger
pointing to the sky,
she tells me to reach for heaven. . . .

Qiana Neff
Grade 10, Crawford High School
Poet-Teacher: Glory Foster
Teacher: Kate Bartels

"Dance of an Angel"
Amy Liao/Grade 8/Muirlands Middle

My Brother's Tempo

From the jazzy wails of Gershwin's "Rhapsody in Blue"
to the classical sound of Mozart's "Symphony No. 9,"
a clarinet's mystical tone weaves its way into my evening practice.
As I play these grand duets over
and over with my brother, Jeff,
reality stops me
and says I've got a long way to go.
But my brother is patient.
He says to keep trying,
that I'll get better each time
until I'm good enough
to play "Trepak"
at his tempo.

Matt Kelly
Grade 6, Hawthorne Elementary
Teacher: Jim Riley
Poet-Teacher: Celia Sigmon

"The Clarinet Dance"
Tara Fuller/Grade 6/Ira Harbison Elementary

Song Wish

Dear Dad,
Hear and bless thy beats
and the bird singers
and gourds with tenderness,
small things that have no words.

I remember when you sang in the car
before you died,
and I can still hear your songs.

Down in the river I can hear you singing.
I run but when I get there I don't see you.
I sit on a rock and wonder who you are.
Then I hear you again. I look around
but only see the sun going down.
I see no one else. Just me, the rocks, the sun and the river.
In the water I see another me. We look at one another.
I hear that song that makes me feel peaceful and alive.
I know who was singing. It was the river, so beautiful.
I wish I could sing like that and be a mystery.

One afternoon, I hear the sound in a well,
so dark I can hardly see.
I touch the water and it feels like
snow falling upon me.
Seeing my reflection,
singing to the water,
hearing how I sound.
The well makes me sound nice.
My singing makes my reflection move,
makes me feel like a feather upon the water,
looking down.

Reina Marie Valadez
Grade 7, Pauma School
Poet-Teacher: Brandon Cesmat
Teacher: Coy Johnston

The Wounded Deer
after a painting by Frieda Kahlo

A deer travels through a dense forest
with the head of a man
and antlers larger than his body.
Without his knowing it
a hunter follows close behind.
The hunter is uglier than the devil himself.
The predator loads a scarlet arrow
lacing it gracefully into his bow.
Releasing the bowstring
with years of experience,
his arrow strikes into the centaur's velvety fur.
Fire burns in his demon eyes.
He loads and fires eight more bright red arrows,
until he realizes he cannot destroy
this figment of his imagination. . . .

Matt Lutes
Grade 7, Mesa Verde Middle School
Poet-Teacher: Glory Foster
Teacher: Daniel Fleming

Sticky History

Stretched open on tar-pit memories
cracked calcium buried beneath aging earth
encompassed by the metal fencing of barriers to children
set free from the restraints of mandatories
children among their parents
unrestricted running on the outskirts of La Brea
stretched open on tar-pit memories
years sealed into box-shaped hearts
melted under the twilight of a hole-punched sky.

Alexis Bittar
Grade 12, Torrey Pines High School
Poet-Teacher: Jim Milner
Teacher: Marie McKittrick

Deer

If I were a deer
I would smell the grass growing
From the heart earth
That always talks
About the silver air
That no one can see.
I would get into a big pool
of fresh, clean water
That is so nice
It lets me in.
I would see the fishes
Swimming in the water
Like sliding into base.
I would dry myself
Shaking my body
I would feel the air
That says to move
Touching my fuzzy legs.
I would feel the water
From the waterfall touching
My fur like the hand of a god holding my
deer hide.

Kota Oe
Grade 3, Torrey Pines Elementary
Poet-Teacher: Steve Garber
Teacher: Brenda Baniaga

""Reaching In the Heart"
Jackie Quach
Grade 10/Morse High

"Twilight City"
Chanelle Hayes/Grade 7/Mesa Verde Middle

Night

The living night
beckons all to come outside
"Take part of the festivities"
Come, watch
    the stars wink
   recalling an old joke
    the moon dances
   bathing in the sleeping sun's warmth
    the trees sing
   to the sounds of the wind blowing through their leaves
And the earth falls awake
to watch the gaiety
that the sky exhibits

Jessica Kondrick
Grade 8, Muirlands Middle
Poet-Teacher: Jana Gardner
Teacher: Wayne Bartos

Pearl Talk

Star
in the dark sky
shines like crystal,
silver as a pearl
of my own talking.
As it shines,
it reminds me of my grandma,
always smiling. Her hair,
her touch as the star's light.
Starface.

Fabiana Hernandez
Grade 8, Pauma School
Poet-Teacher: Brandon Cesmat
Teacher: Laurene Collings

I Am

I am the water rushing down the river.
I am the star who always makes your wish come true.
I am the whale swimming in the ocean.
I am the chicken who is running from the man who wants to kill me.
I am the hungry wolf trying to find food.
I am a crab washed away from the shore.
I am a dog who runs on the plains.
I am the flame of five colors.
I am the moon.
I am the snowman who is skinny.
I am alive.

David Taing
Grade 5, Jackson Elementary
Poet-Teacher: Georgette James
Teacher: Mary Jo Longo

Spiritual Memories

I come
from across a tearful ocean,
from religious persecution
shaping troubles in
"the new land,"
for money,
health,
and happiness.

I come from pain
and suffering
during the Holocaust,
forcing hope and love out of spiritual pleas,
from a family long hurt,
hiding their pain.

I come from long, peaceful walks
in the snow
on a path to freedom,
from moldy ships
and months of aggravation
in intolerable conditions.

I come from a melody of prayers
to stop wrongs
that have never proved right
for the dismal souls
they slaughtered.

I am immigrant hopes
and dreams.

Jordan Laris Cohen
Grade 4, Hawthorne Elementary
Poet-Teacher: Veronica Cunningham
Teacher: Ann MacDonald

"Trail to Nowhere"
Elyse Harthorn/Grade 6/Bonita Vista Middle

Everlasting Journey

A soft flow of water
rushes down the stream.
It looks back on its childhood pictures,
a tiny speck of ice.
It gives its children one final kiss,
then the sun comes out
and their childhood is over.
Immediately they melt down into a strange, cool liquid.
Soon, the sun reaches for their bodies,
and they disappear
on their journey to the clouds.

Sibel Güner
Grade 4, Hawthorne Elementary
Poet-Teacher: Veronica Cunningham
Teacher: Ann MacDonald

Dad

He spoke to me of water
Calling out my name
Out of the deep blue sea
He was calling and calling
Like a wall of water
Hard to pass by
Riding the waves through his life
They carried him up and down

He is of the sky
Like our Father who resides there
Watching over my life
Clouds moving in and out
Brightness and darkness follow him
Changing him with the storms that come and go
Life can be like snow he tells me
As heavy as the wall of an avalanche
Light like fresh fallen snow
No two snowflakes are alike
Enjoy with a sense of wonder
To find pleasure in it that is all my own

He and I are the same
Quiet thinking
Eyes watching
Mouths talking
Hair blowing
Body moving
He is my dad

Geoff Livingston
Grade 5, Torrey Pines Elementary
Poet-Teacher: Steve Garber
Teacher: Anna Lewis

Ear Hunt

What if your head would erase?
You could put your ears together and make a heart.
You could give it to someone for a valentine.
What if you got your ears pierced?
It would look like you had stabbed the heart in half.
What if you bought a teapot?
Put it where your head was and use one ear for a handle
and the other for a cup.
Err, gross. See you later, ear, head.
Oh yeah, and watch out for the earwigs!
What if your ears had insurance?

Carson Kemp
Grade 4, Spreckles Elementary
Poet-Teacher: Tamara Johnson
Teacher: June Pressler Pecchia

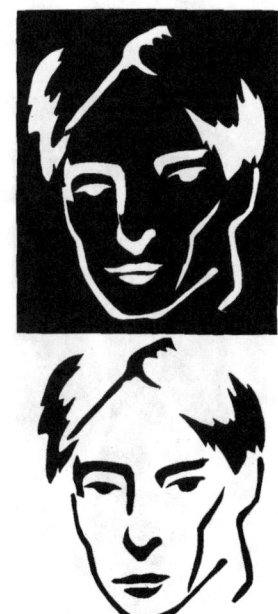

"Thom"
Liza Mendoza/Grade 11/
Morse High

I Hate Book Reports

It's like I'm stunned
in a wrestling match
against The Undertaker.
It feels like he broke my chest.
It feels like I've been in jail
for fifty years.
But the worst part is
I can't watch myself
wrestling
The Undertaker
on TV.

Eyal Florentin
Grade 4, Spreckles Elementary
Poet-Teacher: Tamara Johnson
Teacher: June Pressler Pecchia

*"Shadows Of the Night"
Brian Nicolas/Grade 6/
Valle Lindo Middle*

Jump Word

Words jump from the book
like a big enemy
conquering my head.

Words talk
like a human song
when I see them.

The black word
like a statue
doesn't move
but uses spirits
to talk.

I ate all the words
but nothing is
in my stomach.

Jeff Liao
Grade 7, Mesa Verde Middle
Poet-Teacher: Joe Milosch
Teacher: Kerry Farrar

My Writing

My writing is like mixed-up spaghetti
being tossed around in a bowl,
tangled knots like shoelaces.
When I eat spaghetti,
I think of my writing and
when those tangled knots touch my lips,
they make me think about writing.

Josh Peterson
Grade 4, San Pasqual Union
Poet-Teacher: Brandon Cesmat
Teacher: Victoria Young

Silent Wolf

Why, Wolf, do you look
so strong and big,
yet you glide over
the ground
as if flying?
The wolf stayed silent.
Why do you stay together
when your sister, the fox, goes along?
The wolf is silent.
Why, Wolf, do you howl at the
moon and sing your wild song?
The Wolves are silent.
Why is your pack silent?
You only talk at night, when
you sing your sad song
or when snarling over meat.
Why are you silent?
The wolf answered.
We talk with out tails, our
feet, our bodies, so not to be
heard. We talk a silent language.
We are many colors, white
gray, black, all the colors
of our colorblind rainbow.

Caitlin Morrow
Grade 6, Lindberg/Schweitzer Middle
Poet-Teacher: Claudia Axel
Teacher: Lisa Lee

If I Were a Hippity Hoppity Green Frog

If I were a green frog I would flicker
my tongue to catch insects. I would sit
on a lily pad and have no worries.
I would make a sound like this: "Ribbit, ribbit"
I would live in a pond.
I would hop around like a bouncing ball.
I would have fun getting away from my enemies.

Julianne Golingan
Grade 3, El Toyon Elementary
Poet-Teacher: Johnnierenee Nelson
Teacher Lisa Cohn

The Animal God"
Andrew Becerra/Grade 6/Ira Harbison Elementary

Car Cemetery

The red paint
looks good at night
chipped chrome
glistens under the hum
of neon light

Old man
lonely
snug with grease
sweat stricken pits
in serene atmosphere
keeper of the graveyard

Children, laughing, throw stones

Sam Sundos
Grade 11, Torrey Pines High
Poet-Teacher: Jim Milner
Teacher: Marie McKittrick

"Seatbelts, Please"
Elena Monroe/Grade 8/Bonita Vista Middle

Road Kill
after art by Harrod Blank

The twists of its deadly painted horns
The jagged lines of its bones
Petrify in the scorching sun
Its nostrils flare out puffs of choking smoke
It careens crazily down an old deserted desert highway
Heat builds itself into a flame
On the forehead of the skull
Its teeth are bared and its eyes glare red
Its engine madly roars
The tires peel off the crackling asphalt
With a cry piercing the azure sky
This creature is given life when gasoline
Is poured into its tank
It is the blood that springs it into action
It is no longer an animal
But a raving machine. A bizarre car. . . .

Ryan Beyer
Grade 7, Mesa Verde Middle
Poet-Teacher: Glory Foster
Teacher: Joie Nolasco

Wondrous Things I Have Yet to Understand

I come from the challenge
of my siblings,
from my family's
jumbled mix
of emotions.

I come from the spurring coolness
of the night,
from a healthy lizard,
sunning itself on a rock.

I come from the wonderful season
of newborns and greenery
and from the fierce animals
of the endless prairie.

I come from a world
where mingled wonders
blurt chaos I don't understand.
I come from the bubbles
of the sacred land,
with freckle-faced grasshoppers
leaping through the grass.

Tracy Burnett
Grade 4, Hawthorne Elementary
Poet-Teacher: Veronica Cunningham
Teacher: Ann MacDonald

"The Waking Eye"
Gabriela Campos/Grade 6/Horace Mann Middle

My Eye That's Fly

My third eye is so fly
that all the girls dig him.
He watches stuff that's going on behind me.
At night he goes to the Third Eye Bar
where he hangs out with the other eyes.
In the morning before I wake,
he pops back into my head.
Oh, my eye is fly.
He helps me when my brother
is about to pop me on the back of the head
or steals a twenty from a person's wallet
when I'm talking to them.
My eye pounds people
if they try to beat me up.
The girls really dig that.

John Freeman
Grade 6, Lewis Middle
Poet-Teacher: Tamara Johnson
Teacher: Jamie Walsh

Considering the Spiders

The spiders,
an ugly gray cloudy color,
stringy long legs with
disgusting strands of hairy webs that
stick like gum when I walk into them
because the webs are clear and I can't see them.

Once, I got a good-for-nothing spider
and put him in a jar with my brother's frog,
and with one move that ugly thing was gone,
it made history. I was happy that day.

One evening, a bug was trying to get inside my room.
Then all of a sudden, down flew a spider in a surprise attack.
He missed, but the frightened bug never came back.

For a moment, we looked at each other,
and I sadly remembered the spider that died.
It is in my memory now, and I will remember
the spider who looked at me, forever.

Vanessa Sanchez
Grade 8, Pauma School
Poet-Teacher: Brandon Cesmat
Teacher: Ellen Humphrey

Black Widow

The black widow sulks,
as if her husband has just passed away.
She will strike with her poisonous fangs
if you go near.
She will time your death
with her blood red hourglass.
Her hard tiny body
is dressed in black
as if she has just returned
from a funeral.
She is always expecting,
expecting to find
someone.

Danielle Kleinstuber
Grade 6, The Language Academy
Poet-Teacher: minerva and Jim Milner
Teacher: Helen Peterson

"Black is The Spider"
Esmeralda Rodriguez/Grade 7/Horace Mann Middle

April Fools

The announcement is worn
Gently around the edges.
Yellowed with age and
Crinkly.
My parents looked so
Different
Twenty-two years ago--
Not my parents yet.
My mother wears a Gunny Sack
With a plunging neck line.
She bought it the morning of the wedding,
She tells my romantic ears.
In the picture,
Her smile wavers.
She is nervous, unsure.
She grips my father's large lazy hand
Tightly.
He smiles easily, leaning back in
A hideous polyester leisure suit.
He has a huge curly brown afro.
His smile is true
But his eyes betray him.
This wedding announcement is
The first their parents would hear of it.
A rushed marriage,
Needing a green card,
Afraid of marriage,
But could never part.
They stare at the camera,
On that April 1st afternoon,
Not knowing their life together
Would stretch into a new millennium.

Katie Reynolds
Grade 8, Muirlands Middle
Poet-Teacher: Glory Foster
Teacher: Wayne Bartos

"Tick-Tock-Watch"
Andrew Heiberg/Grade 7/Mesa Verde Middle

To a Mouse

You must have wriggled with joy
when you found that hole in the wall.
You must have squeaked with happiness
when you saw that cheese
on that wood block
like a platter all set out just for you.
How you must have run and
greedily bit into the cheese.
Then "POW!" the metal bar came down.
What a strange death: you lost your head,
but at the same time you got the cheese.
Have you learned your lesson now?

Meredith Snapp
Grade 5, San Pasqual Union
Poet-teacher: Brandon Cesmat

Morning Madness

When I wake up in the morning
my head feels like a bowling ball
my eyes feel like little people are pulling them shut
my arms feel like I'm holding weights
It feels like my mouth is zipped
my hair sticks up like I just got shocked
my feet are still sleeping
It feels like my teeth weigh ninety pounds
I know I am going to have a bad morning

Rachel Dennis
Grade 4, El Toyon
Poet-Teacher: Johnnierenee Nelson
Teacher: Lisa Cohn

"When I Wake Up In the Morning"
Stephanie Eaton/Grade 6/Marston Middle

Morning

When I wake up in the morning
my feet smell like turtles
My leg bones feel like fossils
My arms drag like a gorilla and
my head feels like a dribbled basketball

Miguel Urcino
Grade 6, Marston Middle
Poet-Teacher: Johnnierenee Nelson
Teacher: Andie McCausland

Gray Breath

My hair flows like a river down the back of my head,
like a waterfall.
My fingers are like hatchlings
poking out of their eggs.
My tears are like a summer shower
watering the world below.
My eyes are like two hail rocks.
My hot breath is like a heat wave
moving through the air.
My yell is like a lightning storm.
My breath is like May Gray
on a cold day.
My legs are like poles.
My arms are like two flames from a fire.

Russ Kreeger
Grade 2, San Pasqual Union
Poet-Teacher: Brandon Cesmat
Teacher: Teri MacDonald

The Art of Sky
after art by John Chan

Six blue men
Making wonderful art
By spewing
The great colors of earth
Their bright blue heads
Full of life
Ready for anything

Like a fountain
Paint shooting in all directions
Two painting the earth
A glorious green
Two with the yellow
Sun shooting brightly
Two spitting red
Blood and death

All acting as one
To make an
Immortal picture

The Art of Sky. . . .

Ryan Garcia
Grade 7, Mesa Verde Middle School
Poet-Teacher: Glory Foster
Teacher: Janet Helbock

"Uh Oh"
Kristine Caparino/Grade 7/Mesa Verde

Cloud Laugh

Raindrops
like crystals out of the sky
they hit my shoulders like sharp needles
falling straight into me.
The clouds are laughing as their pointed crystals
crash down on me. All the animals run
into their dens. The raindrops fall, beating down on the flowers,
causing them to wilt, yet
I stand in the middle of all the commotion,
laughing joyfully
in the rain.

Karli Kroeker
Grade 4, San Pasqual Union
Poet-Teacher: Brandon Cesmat
Teacher: Victoria Young

If I Were a Baseball

If I were baseball
I would hear the swoosh
Of the bat
Wait for the smack
Of the wood
Dream of being
A record-breaking
Homerun ball.
If I were a baseball
I would hear the crowd
CHEER
When I went right down the plate
For a strike.
If I were a baseball
I would split the timber
Of the bat
When the pitcher threw a screwball.
I would wait to fly high
In the air when
I touched the
Hardwood bat.
If I were a baseball
I would crumble into
Pieces of leather and soar
With the wicked wind
Hoping to find home.

Daren Rodhouse
Grade 3, Torrey Pines Elementary
Poet-Teacher: Steve Garber
Teacher: Brenda Baniaga

Old White Shoe

An old white shoe
was hanging on the telephone wire
and it was beautiful.
In the night
it's like a little star
and it gives a little bit of light
to the world.

Mohamed Iman
Grade 5, Darnell Elementary
Poet-Teacher: minerva and Jim Milner
Teacher: Sandi Vidana and Barbara Rasmussen

Halloween Magic

Halloween magic
has a sharp tooth
that flys at night
and sucks blood.
It wears a cape
that's red on the inside,
and the outside is
as black as midnight.
In my dream
I am a vampire,
but I give my blood
to the hospitals
for people who need it,
and that's the real magic.

Johnny Thongkham
Grade 4, Lincoln Acres Elementary
Poet-Teacher: Celia Sigmon
Teacher: Adriana Medigovich

A Portrayal of Memories

I come from a world of respect and modesty
Where dresses are worn with itchy underskirts
That rustle when you walk
And the wide ribbon has to be tied
A certain way
Where children may be beaten
If disobedient
Vicious mosquitos
Rule the summers
Snowy winters
Where homes have a courtyard in the center
And everyone is a wonderful artist
The place where my parents left
To bring me in the world
Of English-speaking people
Once my friends were talking of prejudice
I couldn't understand
Their pride
I couldn't believe
Their ignorance
I couldn't stand
Their arrogance
They didn't understand
And probably never will
Maybe it is I who doesn't understand
I am lucky
I was always accepted
But I know those who are never
Because of who they are
I am a daydreamer
I have seen many Disney movies
"Cinderella"
"Sleepy Beauty"
"Snow White"
I dreamed of being the heroine
'Til one day, I woke up from a daydream

And looked in the mirror
I found not the blond princess
Or gorgeous brunette
I saw an Asian girl
I pity my friends for their shallow beliefs
But I envy them also

Karen Kim
Grade 8, Standley Middle
Poet-Teacher: Veronica Cunningham
Teacher: Margaret Joseph

"Dreams in a Bottle"
Eileen Romero/Grade 10/Crawford High

"Heart of Sword: Kenshin"
Aiza Abelon/Grade 11/Morse High

Pearl of the Oriental Sea

You took care of me
for a long time.
You watched over
the things I did.
You used to call me
hard-headed
foolish and over-acting.
You think I don't listen
but I do.
I still hear the stories we shared
and the laughter
the Christmas church songs we sang
like angels we had heard on high.
But our relatives needed help
so you left
and a part of me vanished.
Now, I wait, Grammy.
Me, as foolish as I still am.
Now I wait for
you, hard as stone
falling and climbing hills
because you are
the pearl of the Oriental Sea.

Spencer Amansec
Grade 7, The Language Academy
Poet-Teacher: Celia Sigmon
Teacher: Barbara Davis

What If?

What if
an ocean
of whispers could sing
to rocks that frown
and clouds that
laugh? The pink
sunset would play
with the sad night
that is as cheerless
as the frowning rocks.
Listening stars could
tell me deeds that
only the ocean of
whispers know.

Mark Dy
Grade 3, Las Palmas Elementary
Poet-Teacher: Jana Gardner
Teacher: Ruth Ann Wheatly

Tsunami

If my mother was a tsunami
She would come racing across the ocean towards me
Let me rise on her graceful waves
Towering over all
Telling me of her adventures
We'd drench everything in sight
The ride of my life
My mother would swoop me over buildings
Carry me through the sky
Like a bird
My mother a greenish-blue wall
A great barrier
Teaming with life
Together we would explore
Swallowing up all life
Then we would part
And my mommy
Tsunami
Would drift back to sea

Mackenzie Maher
Grade 5, Torrey Pines Elementary
Poet-Teacher: Steve Garber
Teacher: Anna Lewis

Writing Is Digging

Pencil,
shiny pencil.
I see its pink eraser and brown body just lying here.
I see it in my pencil pouch,
zipped up, squished between the covers.
It is like a worm trying to
get through the dirt of my education.

Becky Espinosa
Grade 7, Hidden Valley Middle
Poet-Teacher: Brandon Cesmat
Teacher: Joanne Brey

"Imagination"
Patrick T. Scott/Grade 4/ Canyon View Elementary

"Misery"
Graciano Avalos/Grade 8/Bonita Vista Middle

Sorrow

Sorrow is a room slowly closing in on you
Everyone feels it at some time
It is an animal trying to break free of a trap, looking
at you with its pleading eyes, praying you will rescue it
Sorrow is a flower that is lifeless and slowly wilting
It is a confused child at a funeral wanting to know when Grandpa's
coming home,
or a mother crying because she is going to die of cancer
leaving all her children motherless
Sorrow is a lake full of tears which some end up drowning in.

Jill Brooks
Grade 7, Mesa Verde Middle
Poet-Teacher: Joe Milosch
Teacher: Joie Nolasco

What Am I?

As black as a starlit sky,
as pallid as a tranquil breeze
    on a sunny morning,
        as thunderous
        as the rain
    on a riverbank,
       as lost
      as a vacant mind,
as green as a gleaming emerald
    in a tropical forest,
      as free
    as a sparkling crane
gliding gracefully through the morning sun,
    as gigantic
     as violins playing,
  as hollow as a sizzling scream,
      a boy
    sitting downhearted
      in school.

Kristopher Bognot
Grade 4, Mason Elementary
Poet-Teacher: Jana Gardner
Teacher: Jody Neiss

Diving Deep

Black makes me feel
like a hocky puck,
like a diver sinking deep in the ocean.
Black happens when the sun drops
into a box or over the edge of the sea.
Black is summer at night
when I imagine myself
floating in the dark sky.

Andres Villa
Grade 4, Lincoln Acres Elementary
Poet-Teacher: Celia Sigmon
Teacher: Adriana Medigovich

Wings That Won't Fly

Restricted to land
You will never soar above
Watching and waiting
Circling over your prey
Instead you slip and glide
Over frosty, glistening ice
Your black eyes
Shine like ebony oblong marbles
As you devour bass
And salty fresh herring
Your webbed feet are sun rays
Cradling an egg
You wait in silent anticipation
For your mate to return
From hunting
Storing up food for the following weeks
Yet you still do not move
Nor retreat to a dark, eerie cave
You wish to rest
But your unborn child
Takes priority over comfort
In the distance you see your mate
And now, Penguin,
You are free. . . .

Erin Dawson
Grade 7, Mesa Verde Middle School
Poet-Teacher: Glory Foster
Teacher: David Sykes

Stoplight Reflected

I turned the street corner and
I heard a woman sobbing, "I can't
do this anymore." Her head tilted against
the lightpost as her tears reflected
sparkling red, green, yellow, rolling
down her burning face.
The crosswalk turned white,
her tears froze with the thought of walking,
taking another chance in this scary world.
But she just stood there as
the light changed over and
over again, reflecting light off her
like pouring rain and lightning.

Mona Safi
Grade 7, Hidden Valley Middle
Poet-Teacher: Brandon Cesmat
Teacher: Jim Hinrichs

"Stop and Imagine"
Faith Elizabeth Becklund
Grade 6/Valle Lindo Elementary

The Ocean Side

In my pink and blue
sea bathing suit
underneath my green shirt
my gray pants
I saw crabs, fish and furious sharks
in the Philippians Sea
the North Pacific Ocean
The sun was shining
all alone in the water
called Cocas Island
a beautiful island with boats floating all around
boats rocking like baby cartels
There I stood like the furious sea
for I have a furious mind and actions

Beth Ann Ahlgren
Grade 5, Torrey Pines Elementary
Poet-Teacher: Steve Garber
Teacher: Anna Lewis

Marian Anderson
after a photo by Richard Avedon

She puckers her lips
in a love song
to herself
Her soul floats
in the serenity
she feels
People stare
and wonder
"Crazy" some remark
turning up their noses
at her
She is shunned
by society
for being
the one
who is different
They laugh at
her large beads
her skin
kissed by the sun
She does not follow
their rules
Her hair is wild
blowing
in a dance of life
"Where is her home?"
They do not believe
she can be happy
without the things they have
Her answer scares them
for their minds are closed
"My home is in my heart
and I am all I need"
she whispers
and then she sings. . . .

Sarah K. Ball
Grade 7, Mesa Verde Middle
Poet-Teacher: Glory Foster
Teacher: Janet Helbock

Black

My favorite color is black
because it is the color of your room
in the night when the door is closed
and you see shadows everywhere
and your only light
is the moon and the stars.

Abel Marquez
Grade 4, El Toyon Elementary
Poet-Teacher: Jill Moses
Teacher: Myrna Kahle

Purple

I am the color purple,
A mist of two opposing sides:
A soft blue baby bow, dainty dress,
Sparkling sapphire, helpful hue;
A hard red crimson cut, hidden heart.
Radiant ruby, contrasting color.

I am the lost haze;
I need identity.
Am I the blue moon?
Am I the red sun?
The flag: red war, blue peace?

Give me the balance, the chance
to shine in the dark world!

Jessica Tiu
Grade 8, Bonita Vista Middle
Poet-Teacher: Johnnierenee Nelson
Teacher: Casey Handrop

I Am

I am a cloud full of little
kids' whispers.
I am the night made of bright
dreams.
A door of stars.
A book of soft
songs.
I am a mirror that
sees a blue ocean of music.
A bird that catches
dreams from a little
baby.
I am eyes made of green
grass.
A door of sadness.
I am lion of popcorn.
A tree full of buzzing
bees.
And a cloud of fiery
smoke.

Margaret Victoria Stenchion
Grade 3, Las Palmas Elementary
Poet-Teacher: Jana Gardner
Teacher: Ruth Ann Wheatley

"The People's Champ"
Patrick Manglinong/Grade 7/Mesa Verde Middle

Listening To The Wind

I am a tiger
that likes to whistle
and dream of dawn
coming over the horizon.
I am blue, a light blue twilight
like an angel's wing.
I am winter, a winter listening
to the wind sizzling in fireworks
on a continent called "Africa,"
a winter that freezes your voice.

Alex Cossio
Grade 3, Lincoln Acres Elementary
Poet-Teacher: Glory Foster
Teacher: Diane Horowitz

The Tiger's Dream

I am a tiger
running around
in a dark red fiery coat
screeching like the wild pig
I just caught.
The pig smells like a good meal
like a juicy steak
just out of the BBQ.
I dream of 7 million pounds
of good steak
shaped like a pyramid.
Then I can climb up on it
and rest and eat
whenever I wake up
on a nice sunny
Friday summer day.

Lance Moore
Grade 6, Valle Lindo Elementary
Poet-Teacher: Glory Foster
Teacher: Pat Neill

Tiger Sky

The tiger is moon light
running through the clouds.
It hunts with its teeth
as bright as jewels.
He runs like a whisper
in the breeze.
His teeth are sharp icicles
in a cold cave.
He sounds like a leaf
blowing in the fall breeze
and flys like a dazzling star.
The tiger is the breath of fire.

Mina Khavari
Grade 4, Canyon View Elementary
Poet-Teacher: Glory Foster
Teacher: Carl Bogucki

"Lion on Ravaged Wings"
Neil Viray/Grade 11/Morse High

My Mom, So Many Things

My mom is like a turtle
because she shelters me.
My mom is like a smile
because when she smiles she's happy.
My mom is like a mountain
because she sets an example
I can see from a long way off.
My mom is like a grassy field
because she is a flower
blossoming pretty and bright.
My mom is like a covered bowl
because that's how I feel
when she hugs me.
My mom is like an eye
because she can see through me.

Jasmine Pikes
Grade 3, Palmer Way Elementary
Poet-Teacher: Glory Foster
Teacher: Melissa Harley

"Coffee Hour"
Jonathan Harthorn/Grade 8/Bonita Vista Middle

Big Shiny Plates

When my mom cleans the kitchen
it smells like fresh bread,
it looks like polished gold.
When she's finished cleaning
she cooks tacos, enchiladas and frioles.
In the cabinet, I see
big shiny plates.
I take one out
and it reflects my face
so clean and bright I can't open my eyes.
I put on my sunglasses
and open my eyes
and ask, "Mom, do you have another plate
that doesn't shine so much?"

Steven Nava
Grade 4, Central Elementary
Poet-Teacher: Glory Foster
Teacher: Christine Calabria

My Tia's Kitchen

In my aunt's kitchen
I remember the fresh smell
of sweet berries
picked right at dawn.
She has a dead plant
so crispy that its skin
crumbles and falls off.
She has a fish in a tank,
as golden as the sun
on a summer's day.
She always asks me
if I want to go out to eat,
but I'm full of roasted chicken.
I will remember her kitchen
because that's where
my first tooth fell out!

Ronald Reza
Grade 5, Lincoln Acres Elementary
Poet-Teacher: Celia Sigmon
Teacher: Susan Braden

The Oldest Rock I Ever Met

My rock was found on a lonely bed
  of empty color.
He is my oldest friend.
His beard touches his endless beating heart.
My rock shares a secret with my soul.
My rock whispers a secret to me.
My rock knows a lot from the passed time
  of his unjoyful life.
I can see and hear his oceanly blue music.
He will even tell a story of his own,
  if you listen harder and harder.

Taylor Waldenmaier
Grade 4, Zamorano Elementary
Poet-Teacher: Veronica Cunningham
Teacher: Carol Neelly

Old Man

Little old man in the mall who has no money to
feed himself. He's a lonely old man who uses
damp newspaper for blankets. I give him
money for food. I tell him, "DON'T
USE THIS MONEY FOR
DUMB THINGS,
PLEASE!"
He smiled at me when
I gave him the money. I rode my bike
for home as fast as the wind, and then when I turned
the corner, he said, "Trust me, I won't," in a thundery voice.

Jacob Peterson
5th Grade, San Pasqual Union
Poet-teacher: Brandon Cesmat
Teacher: Patricia Matson

"My Puzzled World"
Victoria Rosalba Huber/Grade 6/Horace Mann Middle

Globe

The globe is a giant jawbreaker.
I spin to Greenland and it tastes
like peppermint that is really cold and fresh.
I spin to California and it tastes
like grapes that are really sweet.
I spin to Europe and it tastes
like pizza made with melted
cheese, pepperoni and mushrooms,
so I take a slice of Europe
and it's good. Then I go back to Greenland
because the taste of peppermint draws me back.

Norma Resendiz
Grade 5, San Pasqual Union
Poet-Teacher: Brandon Cesmat
Teacher: Christine English

Beneath the Tree

Why does the sun make the peaches fall asleep?
Why does adobe rust and wither with the sun's tears fall upon it?

The peaches sleep on the adobe rust.
The rusty leaves of the peach tree fall to the ground.

Why does the sun shine through the rust to the peaches?
When we sleep beneath a peach tree, why do its leaves swallow us?

Mary Ann Gaudreault
Grade 7, Hidden Valley Middle
Poet-Teacher: Brandon Cesmat
Teacher: Jim Hinrichs

"A Peaceful Flower in the World"
Kristine Kae T. Palamos/Grade 3/Palmer Way Elementary

Bursting Bees

Bursting bees
so yellow like daisies and
the stripes so black like the night sky.

Garrison Williams
Grade 2, San Pasqual Union
Poet-Teacher: Brandon Cesmat
Teacher: Stacy Turner

Orange Trees

The orange trees in my yard are full
of sweet smelling blossoms in the summer.
In one tree there is a golden-white, smooth
bee hive. The bees hum around it crazily,
madly. When the oranges are ripe, I will
pick them to take to my mom for juice.
My cats come to sun their thick
coats of fur. Suddenly they are alert,
their mysterious eyes darting from one
side to the other like pendulums, watching
the movement of wild birds darting about.
There I stand by the door in the morning,
watching all this watching with a secret sunny smile

Rachel Paarman
Grade 5, San Pasqual Union
Poet-Teacher: Brandon Cesmat
Teacher: Patricia Matson

Wonder Water

Waiting for morning to come
Waiting for the moment when light and dark touch
Get up for a fresh start
Sprinklers splash everywhere
Wetting the grass
Matting down wet
Soggy leaves covering the ground
The dark brown bark of the tree
Smudged with water
Like a painting
Crystal water
Shining like a rainbow
Sparrows chirrup together
Filling the air with enchanting music
The day is moody, temperamental
Children laugh
Making their bellies hurt
Sitting in the sprinklers as the day disappears
Dusk arrives
Turning the sky rosy red
They fall asleep anxiously
Awaiting the dance of dreams

Mackenzie Maher
Grade 5, Torrey Pines Elementary
Poet-Teacher: Steve Garber
Teacher: Anna Lewis

"Sun, Moon and Stars"
Garret Pace/Grade 7/Mesa Verde Middle

Samoran Night

Night in Samora, Michocan, Mexico.
Dark and lonely
when you could hear leaves fall.
Lonely as space and as quiet as the woods.
I saw an old man on the street as
lonely as a boy without his mom.
Everyday, the old man went to The Coffee Inn and
drank coffee in the dark and lonely night.
He always wore his jewelry.
He was waiting for his love,
but the woman of his dreams never came
to the old man at the lonely Coffee Inn.

Jose Jauregui
Grade 8, San Pasqual Union
Poet-Teacher: Brandon Cesmat
Teacher: Linda Greenwood

"The Essence of Light"
Emily Richards/Grade 7/Mesa Verde Middle

Twilight

I sit on a large wide sandstone rock
high on a hill above my valley, yet not at the top.
The rock ripples like flowing water that froze
    casting shadows inches short,
        millenniums long.

Gold and copper light comes over the hills
and trees to warm the rock I sit on.
Little swirls and ripples turned to stone
for all time. I still feel it flowing.

Lorraine Munoa
Grade 7, San Pasqual Union
Poet-Teacher: Brandon Cesmat
Teacher: Linda Greenwood

Shy

I feel shy because I have to give a report in front of the class,
but my stomach gets butterflies and my head hurts.

Because I have to translate for my dad,
I get nervous and scared.

Because when someone is on the phone in ingles,
I have to talk what the person is talking

what he wants, they tell me
what he wants. Because he wants to talk with his friend,

I feel shy.

Berenice Ledesma
Grade 5, San Pasqual Union
Poet-Teacher: Brandon Cesmat
Teacher: Christine English

A Bright Yellow Room

The baby's room
is yellow and bright.
The pillow and crib are soft.
Beanie Babies are everywhere,
and so are some bears.
There are lots of books
on the shelf and I
am standing here by myself. . . .
All alone.
Waiting for the new baby
to be born.

Mia Legaspi-Cavin
Grade 4, Canyon View Elementary
Poet-Teacher: Glory Foster
Teacher: Renie Martin

My Mom's Hands

My mom's hands fed me,
brushed my hair, dressed me,
held me, put me to bed
so she could do what she
needed to do--clean the house,
make food so I could eat.
And she still does all these things.
Now that I'm big, she goes
to work making cheesecakes
with her small, little-girl hands.
After work, her hands are sore
so I massage them. I see
lines, I see the shape of an "M"
in her palm. They're soft
but sometimes rough
because they are working hands,
Mexican hands. I like my mom's
hands so much.

Cristobal Garcia
Grade 9, Chula Vista High
Poet-Teacher: Jim Milner
Teacher: Jonathan Barns

"Within Our Reach"
Cristy Rodriguez/ Grade 8/Bonita Vista Middle

Beautiful Hands

My mom's hands have long fingernails.
My mom's hands are making tortillas.
It sounds like falling raindrops.
The hands of my mom look
like the wings of a bird.
I ask, "What are you doing?"
She turns around and smiles
saying, "Do you want to help me?"
I say, "Yes," and start patting tortillas too. . . .

Claudia Haman
Grade 3, Kimball Elementary
Poet-Teacher: Glory Foster
Teacher: Bene Calderon

Crazy Cat Girl

Crazy eternal Cat Girl
Arriba
Magenta underwear
Funky chicken
Dancing to disco
Shaking her feathered tail
Crazy Cat Girl
With a bad hair day
And magenta pants
Jumping like a spazz
Is a spazz
Is a raspberry
Growing
On a blueberry bush
A purple Pizzazz Pinata
Filled with crimson frogs
And chartreuse jalapenos
Doing the macarena
The chicken dance
The chicken dancing
Macarena Jalapeno
Night club dance
Dance the night away
Fireworks tonado
Spinning
Setting Ricky Martin's
Head on fire
Vocal Spaghetti
Wrapped around a chunk
Of the sky
A piece of craziness
Lands in your pants
And makes you
Dance
A loony goony dance
Across the kitchen floor
As twilight disappears
Into dawn
Arriba
Crazy Cat Girl. . . .

Destini Digiorgio
Grade 7, Mesa Verde Middle School
Poet-Teacher: Glory Foster
Teacher: Joie Nolasco

My Cat

is the blue, peaceful ocean.
He is a lazy day.
My cat is a flute's melody,
a meadow full of wildflowers.
He is a monkey, a skillful climber.
My cat is my dessert.

Amy Wills
Grade 4, Mason Elementary
Poet-Teacher: Jana Gardner
Teacher: Jody Neiss

"Learning How to Fish and Learning How to Swim Faster!"
Bianca Maldonado/Grade 6/Valle Lindo Elementary

"Winter"
Yandy Palenzuela/Grade 6/Valle Lindo Elementary

Backyard of Books

A story is a lot of socks stacked up high in the air.
A story is like little people on paper.
A ten-page story is like ten ties.
A story is like a flag.
A story is like a backyard
because it's flat and you can play on it.

Jimmy Orduno
3rd Grade, San Pasqual Union
Poet-teacher: Brandon Cesmat
Teacher: Tim Harmon

Winter Landscape

My sister is the winter moon
She eclipses the sun with her soft white light
She guides me through the crumbling moss of nightmares

My sister smells like the mist of canyons
She laughs like the light that floods a greenhouse atrium
She cries like shadows in a field filled with sharp grass
Her hair is black seaweed that
Tango in the rough waves of the ocean

Crossing the brilliant white wilderness
She leaves her footprints in the wet snow
Sepia colored memories fill my hands
And sift through my fingers like grains of sand

But light can travel even across the empty space
"I see the moon, and the moon sees me"
In a dimension where yesterday and today embrace each other
Sometimes the moon rises in the morning
Sometimes the moon swims inside the sea

As the gentle clouds melt into the solitary sky
Together we watch the universe accelerate
At the speed of leaves falling off poplar trees

Masumi Taketomi
Grade 11, La Jolla High
Poet-Teacher: Jill Moses
Teacher: Robin Visconti

The Flying Sneeze

My body is the street.
My fingers are cars.
My head is a museum.
When people come to me,
I feel important.
My legs are meadows.
My eyes are parks.
My ears are farms.
My mouth is a pool.
My nose is a tree. Once,
a bird landed on my nose.
His feathers tickled my nose, and I sneezed.
Everything went flying. Then,
after a week, I was fixed.

        Kendall Plant
        Grade 2, San Pasqual Union
        Poet-teacher: Brandon Cesmat
        Teacher: Teri MacDonald

Anger

Anger seems black as darkness and red
like a wild bull.
I hear it growling like a mad dog.
I smell its red fire
anger tastes like a
dead fish.

        Jeremy Shivick
        Grade 8, Bonita Vista Middle
        Poet-Teacher: Johnnierenee Nelson
        Teacher: Casey Handrop

Howling

My spine is a cat.
In my heart, a dog is howling.
My legs are strong bones
like trees.

Baneza Aguilar
Grade 1, San Pasqual Union
Poet-Teacher: Brandon Cesmat
Teacher: Francis Juarez

"Full Moon"
Jordan Gaviola/Grade 6/Ira Harbison Elementary

I Am a Shadow

I am the wind of white whispers

                I am the fog of red fires

I am the sun of pink love

                I am the Santa Ana of blue sadness

I am a shadow
A shadow of a memory of everything
In a blink of a second when you remember
Reach down into your heart
And your soul
Find me--pull me out
And look through all the memories you lost
That blink of a second seems to last forever.

Sarah Shearer
Grade 4, La Jolla Elementary
Poet-Teacher: Jana Gardner
Teacher: Barbara Rodenrys

"No One Is Ever Whole"
Katherine Caimol/Grade 10/Morse High

The Song of Loss

The grief of loss as I watched things leave over and over:
when I stepped onto the porch four years ago
to notice our pet frog missing,
as I watched the baseballs magically plummet
into the thick bushes,
poker chips zooming through the air like flying saucers
soon lost near the stairs.

I also greeted the lesson of loss
as it threw away cold after cold,
my fevers evaporating like a glass of water in the desert,
the matter of strenuous homework
going away when I'd dealt with it;
bruises and bumps dissolving into thin air,
red pain growing older and drier until it falls
limply on the ground.

As the years pass, I thank loss
and curse it,
my mind accepting it as a normal life.

Akio Mitsunaga
Grade 3, Hawthorne Elementary
Poet-Teacher: Veronica Cunningham
Teacher: Ann MacDonald

I Believe Beautiful Things

I believe roses are
beautiful
like shooting stars
crossing the dark
navy blue sky
in the middle
of the night
with crowds of people
coming outside their
homes to watch them.
I believe my dad
loves my mom like
a sweet juicy fig in his mouth
his teeth and tongue helping him
make a thin rip between the coat of
the fig so more juice can come spraying out
into his mouth.
I believe my mom loves me
like mama bear loves her cub
holding him tight in her big strong paws
telling him not to be scared of the dark loud thunder
blasting into the beautiful forest.
I believe the sky is beautiful
like a garden growing its beautiful
white, pink and violet roses in the spring
with birds coming out of their nests
singing their lovely songs.

Nicole Flores
Grade 4, Torrey Pines Elementary
Poet-Teacher: Steve Garber
Teacher: Richard L. Berry

"Love"
Katie Pearson/Grade 8/
Bonita Vista Middle

The Petals of the Rose

I believe my friends are like rose petals
Drifting through a meadow
A gust of wind comes
Picks up the petals
Scoops them into the air
They dance cartwheels and summersaults
My eyes are dazzled by the floating ballerinas
At sunset the breeze tucks the petals back onto their stems
As the children of the town fold into their beds
The rose folds into its bed

Meryn Beckett
Grade 4, Torrey Pines Elementary
Poet-Teacher: Steve Garber
Teacher: Richard L. Berry

If I Were an Ocean

If I were an ocean
I would hear my crashing waves at the shore
Expressing wild feelings, listening for the call of the whales
Ready to welcome them
I would smell the salty air gathering by my waters
Watch the dolphins playing at my shore splashing
And diving I would grow
To be all of the earth with life leaking out
Into space, my waves would fly up into the sky
Calling out
Their song crumbing into a ripple gliding along the shore
Hearing the sounds of crackling sand
I would let my soul ride
A seahorse through the ocean

Delaney Maher
Grade 3, Torrey Pines Elementary
Poet-Teacher: Steve Garber
Teacher: Brenda Baniaga

"My Sunlight"
Alyssa Ancheta/Grade 10/
Morse High

Misty Bay

Because the mist and fog in the downtown morning
made the ships in San Diego Bay look like they were on fire,

and because everything was damp and foggy and
the roar of the jets coming into the airport and cars going to work,

the crabs just coming out from under the rocks and
my dog growling at them,

the traffic getting bigger, the city buses loading up,
the sails of The Star of India sticking out of the fog,

and because the boats left from the dock
and the fish jumped out of the water,

I write. . . .

> **Andrew Stuck**
> Grade 4, San Pasqual Union
> Poet-Teacher: Brandon Cesmat
> Teacher: Wendy Snapp

Don't Need No Ketchup or Mayonnaise

Kill that spider!
Smash it! Wipe it up!
across the Pacific
that could've been lunch
caterpillars, ants, they eat'em alive
when you got an appetite
who needs insecticide
grilled, broiled, even deep-fried
just munch on a stink bug
and My Oh My!
you'll be thrown in a world
of flavor and taste
don't need no ketchup, don't need mayonnaise
but sure for a while
your breath will smell bad
but after a bit, I know you'll be glad
so come on over
anywhere overseas
sit your butt down
and we'll have a bug feast. . . .

Jansen Cudal
Grade 10, Morse High School
Poet-Teacher: Glory Foster
Teacher: Mary Scanlon

"Cow Dreams"
Cassandra Opel/Grade 10/Morse High

Happiness

Happiness is a bird
that sings wildly all day long
It is a mirror
that reflects what you want to see
It is is a lake
full of fish, boats and people
Happiness is a child
getting a brand new toy
Happiness is a flower
blooming brightly in the forest
It is a dog wagging his tail joyfully
Happiness is a heart pumping
rapidly like a running tiger

Dustin Crawford
Grade 5, Valley Vista
Poet-Teacher: Johnnierenee Nelson
Teacher: David Casdan

Popcorn

A golden droplet of water
tumbles and drops.
When joined by others,
its perfection multiplies
into a field of blooming white roses.

Jenny Feng
Grade 9, University City High
Poet-Teacher: Tamara Johnson
Teacher: Sally Owen

"Nature's Gift"
Tien Le/Grade 7/Mesa Verde Middle

The Fog's Playground

        If I was fog I would make
people turn on their lights
        If I was fog the sun
could not stop me
        If I was fog I would cool
off the world
        And the street would
be my playground
        I would make the clouds
jealous
        I would come in
stuttering whispers
        If I was fog I would make
you rub your eyes
        If I was fog I would be
the cause of accidents
        And be the blanket
wrapped around you
        When you don't want
to get out of bed
        If I was fog I would make
the wind chimes sing
        If I was fog I would be
the summer rain storm
everyone complains about

Meg Felix
Grade 7, Mesa Verde Middle
Poet-Teacher: Glory Foster
Teacher: Marycay Densmore

"Town Of Love"
Christian Lorenzo/Grade 4/
Central Elementary

The Gift

As I walked into my room
I saw that Buck, my cat,
Was standing on my bed.
A half-eaten, bloody lizard
Was on my pillow.
It was about a foot-and-a-half long.
I looked down at Buck.
He blinked affectionately.
Kneeling down, I patted him
On his stripped orange head,
And his purr got even louder.
His wet nose pressed against mine.
An hour later, I had my dad
Dispose of the thing.
It was a wonderful gift.

Lizanne Koch
Grade 5, Hawthorne Elementary
Poet-teacher: Celia Sigmon
Teacher: Jim Riley

A One-Of-A-Kind Design

My mom is like a windmill
blowing away all my sorrow.
My mom is like a star
shinning brightly making me feel proud.

My mom is a one-of-a-kind design
on a sand dollar, very unique.
My mom is like a ballerina's dress
comfortable to wear and talk to.

She is like an airplane's propeller
winding up to tell me my punishment.
That's my mom...

She smells very sweet
Like a bed of lilacs in the spring.

She's the color of a brown-stemmed flower.
Her hair is as black as night.
His eyes are as brown as my leather watchband.

She's very fragile yet strong in her heart.
That's my Mom...

Jami Heard
Grade 6, Horace Mann Middle
Poet-Teacher: Glory Foster
Teacher: Vini Decker-Wells

Sadness Is a Million Bee Stings

My great-grandpa was like a sea urchin
once colorful, bright and happy.
His love was as large as the deep blue sea
and his kindness as big as a hill.
His mind was like the Spiral Nebula
of the Milky Way; he always gave
warmth with his hugs like a fluffy cookie
just coming out of the oven.
Every time I had to leave him
my sadness stung like a million bees.
It seemed as if I was a pin cushion stabbed
with needles, or a boulder had hit me in the stomach.
Although he is gone, his memory stands
as tall as a mountain that I can see
from a million miles away. His love still
explodes like an erupting volcano.
This was my great-grandpa.

Lisa Carbone
Grade 7, Mesa Verde Middle
Poet-Teacher: Glory Foster
Teacher: Terry Heck

"Smile Now, Cry Later"
Nathan Hidinger/Grade 6/Valle Lindo Elementary

Loneliness

Loneliness is a fragile dandelion growing on a
New York sidewalk swallowed in exhaust
It is a rainbow trout bounding up a sewage spout
It is a seven-year old teddy bearless child
in a less than mild airport on Thanksgiving
It is an Artic critter in a sizzling sea of kitty litter
It is an honest farmer wearing a muskrat hat
in a crowd of thieving bureaucrats
It is a fat, fluff house cat named Dare
chased by a herd of diamon-hoofed angry mares
It is a tree struggling to grow
on the lip of a high cliff.

Carolyn Turner
Grade 8, Horace Mann Middle
Poet-Teacher: Johnnierenee Nelson
Teacher: Cheryl La Fond

Crutches

Crutches look like fins
on a whale or fish in
the blue sandy wet sea where
all the fish swim so fast that
scales fall from the fins like
sparks from fireworks.

Aaron Primm
Grade 4, San Pasqual Union
Poet-Teacher: Brandon Cesmat
Teacher: Christine English

"Piranha"
Jorieth Jose/Grade 12/Morse High

The Sea

       The black sea
sings me to sleep at night.
The sand is my blanket
of goose feathers.
Rocks are little old men
gray and sad.
Reflections of the moon dance
in my eyes where they sleep.
Oaks whisper,
       Shhhhh. . . .
Do you hear them?
Giant oaks are whispering my name.
Squirrels are calling me, too.
Blue jays sing me a song.
Gigantic gray rocks
talk to me, keeping me safe.
The river rapids chant a lullaby
telling me secrets,
       Shhhhh. . . . You are the song.
       Shhhhh. . . . You are the dancer.
       Shhhhh. . . . You are the sea. . . .

Melissa Duenas
Grade 6, Ira Harbison Elementary
Poet-Teacher: Glory Foster
Teacher: Linda Cartwright

Piano Joys

You let out gales of laughter
as my fingers tickle your teeth.
You let out your agony
when I pound wrong notes through your system.
Little hammers tap and pound the strings that make up your senses.
You grow old as your voice crackles and its pitch changes.
You have three metal feet
polished smooth by people constantly stepping on them
as they play out the songs written on the creamy sheets
resting in your eyes. You grasp the paper with lines and spots,
not the music until we have pounded and tickled your teeth.

Erika Palmer
Grade 6, San Pasqual Union
Poet-Teacher: Brandon Cesmat
Teacher: Lisa Van Plew

My Family

My mom is as mean as a lion
My dad is a clown
as funny as Goofy
My sister is nasty mud
My cousin, J.J., is as rude as a buffalo
I am as cute as a beautiful calico kitten.

Millie Angela Umali
Grade 3, Las Palmas
Poet-Teacher: Johnnierenee Nelson
Teacher: Ida Gordon

The Blues

Blue is the color of a morning flower
the sky with clouds, its highest towers.
Blue is the color of the ocean at night
and birds when they first take flight.
The feeling of sadness deep inside
when your little sister has cried.
Blue is the color of a beautiful sapphire
and the bright future to which you aspire.
Blue is the color of cold, sad, winter
and also a man named Mr. Flinter.
Blue is the color of blueberry pie
and a man who just flew right by.
Blue is the most beautiful color of all
the seasons: spring, summer, winter, or fall.

Kristen Love
Grade 4, Canyon View Elementary
Poet-Teacher: Glory Foster
Teacher: Renie Martin

"The Popping Of Chaos"
Leigh Anne Silverio/ Grade 11/Morse High

Dancing with my Grandmother

I lay awake in the dark night
Thinking about my grandmother
Who passed away the weekend before school ended.
She was proper as she gracefully walked
With her back straight
To the glossy dance floor
To teach me the box step.
I learned quickly, as we danced together.
Each lesson I would run to her pale
Stretched-out arms
As she greeted me with a warm
"How are you?"
She really wanted to know.

Dallis Fox
Grade 5, Hawthorne Elementary
Poet-Teacher: Celia Sigmon
Teacher: Jim Riley

""Chaotic Love"
Sheena Deguzman/Grade 10/Morse High

My Mom's Sewing Room

My mom has telas
in her sewing room,
and these fabrics are dancing
and hopping around.
I like it when they flap and spin.
And here's a little secret.
Sometimes I dance with them.

Aurelia Alicia Arroyo
Grade 4, Lincoln Acres Elementary
Poet-Teacher: Celia Sigmon
Teacher: Adriana Medigovich

Watermelon Eyes

When I wake up my eyes are
shut like a watermelon
my mouth is dry like the desert
my legs and arms feel like someone
dropped rocks on them
my toes feel like ice cubes
my fingers feel like french fries and
my hair feels as spiky as a cactus

Jeanette Ramirez
Grade 4, Valley Vista Elementary
Poet-Teacher: Johnnierenee Nelson
Teacher: Rose Lucero

A Kitchen Perfumed with Spices

I see my mother's kitchen.
Her kitchen, with the brown tile floor
the green metal sink
the grumbling burgundy refrigerator
the faded wood cabinets
and the yellow light
burning dimly over everything.
My mother's kitchen is a blending
of all the soft essential colors of the earth.
Her kitchen perfumed with spices
with a slow roasting lamb in the oven
with crushed garlic melting
into buttered French bread
with oregano in peppermint sauce.
My mother's kitchen fragrance
is overpowering, but wonderful.
Her kitchen with the constant soft sounds
the clatter of pans, running water,
and the click of her footsteps.
I see, smell, hear,
the symphony of her room, her kitchen.

Elspeth Miller
Grade 10, Morse High School
Poet-Teacher: Glory Foster
Teacher: Robert Lunsford

"Summer Days"
Kelli Carroll/Grade 4/Spreckels Elementary

Spring Day

I was standing there tall and strong
when all the green grass
gathered around me.

People's hands were on me
and little red, almost-round
balls were hanging down from me.

I felt the water down under me and
I felt the hot sun shining down at me,
but I stood still and enjoyed it

because I was an apple tree.

Phuong Pham
Grade 8, Wangenheim Middle
Poet-Teacher: minerva
Teacher: Susan Lundmark

Silent Hill Nocturne

Silent Hill is a deserted town.
The moon is barely visible through dense fog.
You can barely see the road.
The sound of wild, skinned dogs rip the scene up.
Shadows in Silent Hill stalk you.
The sound of beating wings is everywhere.
Snow is unbearably cold in Silent Hill as
it falls mysteriously out of season.
Stores and houses are empty.
Empty cars line the streets and
the roads end in black holes.

Nathan Torian
Grade 7, San Pasqual Union
Poet-Teacher: Brandon Cesmat
Teacher: Linda Greenwood

"Midnight Slumber"
Karen Lopez/Grade 10/Morse High

Medicine Bag

In my medicine bag is a rock
with paisley circle shapes,
black as the starry night
with white freckles.
You can't break it,
since it's used for strength.
There's also a hummingbird egg
small as a school eraser
and the color of milky white.
The power of every egg is different,
like every person is different.
I have a dark emerald
the size of a beer cap
that holds the power of beauty.
All these I keep
in a leather bag
that holds strong things
so their powers won't escape.
But if they do,
they will go back to my mind
because they're all kept in my head.

Jasmine Lopez
Grade 4, Gage Elementary
Poet-Teacher: Celia Sigmon
Teacher: Laurie Hill

I Believe

I believe everyone can learn.
Like nestlings
we must try to fly.
I believe we should
have no homework.
Like the rain
we must stop sometime.
I believe we should write more
in class.
Our stories are windows
into our souls.
I believe in everyone
that they have at least
one good point
like a mischievous puppy.
I believe in children
that we should have more voice
in what happens around us
a storm of thought
followed by thunder
when we speak.
I believe that we should preserve
our world
like a beaver
the world its dam.

Caitlin Sussman
Grade 4, Torrey Pines Elementary
Poet-Teacher: Steve Garber
Teacher: Richard Berry

"Coaxing Love"
Stefanie Miller/Grade 7/Mesa Verde Middle

The Color of Loneliness
for Bobby Lea Taylor II

Red is the blood dripping from him
Red is the passion keeping him alive
Red is the danger he faced
Blue is the sorrow my Mom felt that day
Blue is my lonely feeling
Blue is how I feel when I think of my Step Dad
White is the death we knew would come
White is so pure, yet so sad
White is the way he went
White is the dove soaring
Now that he's gone
Blue, I feel blue with out my Step Dad
Red is the way hope faded
White is so pure, yet so sad. . . .

Heather Ann Smith
Grade 6, Horace Mann Middle
Poet-Teacher: Glory Foster
Teacher: Vini Decker-Wells

The Turtle

There was nothing in the desert
except for a turtle moving slowly across
the desert floor.
The turtle was as lonely as a criminal
locked up for life within his cell.
The turtle was as dry as the sun,
and looked as old as a great-grandfather,
and fragile as an old lady with spindly legs.
Yet the turtle's shell was as hard as titanium
and his mouth filled with razor sharp teeth.

Martin Perez
Grade 10, Chula Vista High
Poet-Teacher: Jim Milner
Teacher: Jonathan Barns

"Eating Lizard"
Jonny Vance/Grade 4/Canyon View Elementary

If I Were a Caterpillar

If I were a caterpillar
I would dream of fluttering through the air, a beautiful butterfly
Climbing trees and eating luscious, red, ripe apples
Because they taste so juicy
I would crawl through the meadows
With the grass tickling my tummy
Eating the bright green clovers
I would meet with my frog friends
Try croaking for a while
I'd play chase with some birds
Letting them think they were going
To get some dessert
I would eat some more
Get nice and plump
After that, I would start my important climb
Of transformation
Up a tree
Where I'll make my chrysalis
There I would wait
Wait a long time
In the end
I would fly away
In the direction of the rainbow
As a beautiful mammoth butterfly

Anthony Randall
Grade 3, Torrey Pines Elementary
Poet-Teacher: Steve Garber
Teacher: Brenda Baniaga

Great-Great-Grandfather

The kids called him Old Gizzer.
They called him Old Man.
He walked from Culiacan
and left by the beach.
He came with only $1000
in his pockets that he'd
saved for two years.
If he went through all that trouble
I guess he really wanted
a better life for himself and his family.
If they only knew
what he went through
to get here, I think
they would give him more respect.
But, too late. He's dead
and in heaven, young and strong.
If they could only see him now.
I don't think they'd call him
Old Gizzer any more.

Orlando Garcia
Grade 7, The Language Academy
Poet-Teacher: Celia Sigmon
Teacher: Barbara Davis

The Oldest Thing in the World

The oldest thing in the world
is a grandpa.
He does not smell.
He feels soft
and he is kind.

Ian Philip Tapang
Grade 3, Palmer Way,
Poet-Teacher: Johnnierenee Nelson
Teacher: Melissa Harley

"The Big Feast"
Victor Ravago/Grade 6/Horace Mann Middle

The Failure

The Failure
To conquer
Our animalistic instincts
Draws forth
Our deepest thoughts
To emerge
And purposefully hurt
Those we consider
Inferior.
Our failure
Shaped the bully.

Michiyo Wellington-Oguri
Grade 8, Standley Middle
Poet-Teacher: Veronica Cunningham
Teacher: Margaret Joseph

"Reflection Lake"
Miles Wallio/Grade 5
Valle Lindo Elementary

Frozen In Time
after a painting by Ethel Green

I stand
By the water's edge
Changed
Hammered
Sawed
Packed
Molded
Beaten
Into the shape
Of my former slave
I stare
Deep, deep into the frozen pond
Frozen in time
I see a person
Egg in hand
The remnants of
My old self
I turn my head
I see a person
With egg in hand
Looking deep
Boring holes into the shape it used to be
Behind us
Stands the tree
Bursting with enormous white fried-egg flowers
A mountain
Stands behinds us all
But the tree is still there
Grown from an egg
Like a green chick
Sprinkled with daises
In its hair
The egg
The pearl white egg
Brings life
and death. . . .

Victoria Ryan
Grade 7, Mesa Verde Middle
Poet-Teacher: Glory Foster
Teacher: Janet Helbock

Poet-One, Poetry-Nothing

Poetry is a wrestling match.
You pull up your spandex,
put on your helmet,
pull up your knee pads,
and tie your shoes.
It's time to enter the mat.
You fight
to win the words in your mind.
Trying to kill,
to be dead-on,
so you can entertain the crowd.
You pull, you push
to be on top of the word.
Your coach calls,
"Get the half!"
"Get the cradle!"
Only to find the word
beginning to get up,
get away.
You tuck it in,
suck it up,
and shoot at him,
only to find he sprawls.
Both you
and your opponent,
are tired...
Your poem is almost over.
Your sweat, your blood,
are now the only reason

to win!
To hear the cheers.
To hear the shouting fans.
To prove yourself.
Your last shot,
you shoot...
Strike true!
You get the cradle
hold on.
Pin!
One, two, three!
You win the match,
the poem is done.

Richard Hess
Grade 10, Morse High School
Poet-Teacher: Glory Foster
Teacher: Robert Lunsford

"In Criminal's Hands"
Doug Brown/Grade 7/Mesa Verde Middle

My Mother is a Tornado

This conch shell is like my
mother. Her voice is like
the ocean splashing
against the rocks.
When she walks
she twirls like a
dancer. When
she talks her
voice is a
deep cave.
Her favo-
rite outfit
is purple
like
grapes
When
I do
some
thing
wrong
she's
sharp
as a
sword.
When
she
cleans
she
spins
like a
tornado.
When
she hugs
me she's
roomy
as our
living
room couch

Jorges Vidales
Grade 4, Central Elementary
Poet-Teacher: Glory Foster
Teacher: Linda Goodman

"Sun Demons"
Sheila Thomas/Grade 4/Canyon View

Grandfather

Looking like an old piece of granite stone,
Sounding like the roar of thunder across the clouds,
My grandfather.

Michael Haider
Grade 7, The Language Academy
Poet-Teacher: Regina Morin
Teacher: Linda Goodman

For the Last Time
after a painting by Monet

Shattered memories
Are no longer visible
Hidden by the dust
Squeezed into the cracks
And stuffed
Beneath the couch cushions
I close this door behind me
For the last time
I close it
On all my memories
On the past
My life
This part
Of me

Kimberly Cruikshank
Grade 7, Horace Mann Middle
Poet-Teacher: Glory Foster
Teacher: Rebecca Koskinen

"The Tumbler"
Allen Isabelo/Grade 10/Morse High

Jasmine Mayo's Complete Guide To Survival

Only say "I love you" when you really mean it
Memories live forever
There is no such thing as superstition
only gullibility
Fate exists
Never would I molest another girl
guys are a different story
Art and culture are doors to a new
amazingly different world
it is open to everyone
but entered by few
Cover your mouth when you cough
Suicide is not an option
ever
Live without regret
but don't break your promises
Don't try your best
do your best
People think extreme superficiality and materialism
in our society is trendy
I think it's shallow, hypocritical, dookie
I would never run through a whole video naked
The pen will forever be mightier than the sword
The pen is mightier is the best solution
to fixing "disabled" men
I believe in true unconditional love
I think the khaki-a-go-go dance
is the best innovation to ever grace
the television screen
Music today is in a long artistic stagnation
I would never do any type of drug for a "high"
and no matter what a stripper says
there's no sex in the champagne room.

Jasmine Mayo
Grade 12, Morse High School
Poet-Teacher: Glory Foster
Teacher: Robert Lunsford

In the Shadows

If I was a shadow
I would scare the world
If I was a shadow
I would walk on the wall
And be a friend of light
If I was a shadow
I would take the form of any structure
Or mimic the original
If I was a shadow
I couldn't get hurt
If I was a shadow
I would feel like the air
And taste like salt
Smelling of decay
If I was a shadow
I would sound like the wind
If I was a shadow
I would sound like the wind
If I was a shadow
I would look like death. . . .

Christian Banzon
Grade 7, Mesa Verde Middle School
Poet-Teacher: Glory Foster
Teacher: Marycay Densmore

Little Dragon of Sorry Ghosts

Patches of color burning softly
in the wondrous window
filling the air
with a flickering breath
sharing rage
with the heavens
for a soul
trapped
inside an
everlasting lamp.

Carissa Perkins
Grade 3, Hawthorne Elementary
Poet-Teacher: Veronica Cunningham
Teacher: Ann MacDonald

Mysteries from the Soul

Flickering hundreds of times per second,
Your wings send a thrill
of adventure into mystified minds.
Your neck flashing like a cherry red ruby
back and forth, flower to flower.
Your long jet-black beak
sucks plentiful nectar
all day long.
With sudden movement
violent purple tail feathers
arise among splashes of color.
A lonely little hummingbird,
Perched atop the world. . . .

Steven Burningham
Grade 7, Mesa Verde Middle School
Poet-Teacher: Glory Foster
Teacher: Marycay Densmore

"Heavenly Bliss"
Vanessa Panaligan/Grade 12/Morse High

Space

White stars
like a million candles
shining down.
Asteroids, comets, meteors
like flying giants.
Mercury
like the desert.
Venus
the planet of love.
Mars
planet of mystery.
Jupiter
immense and foggy.
Earth
the planet of life.
The home I live on. . . .

Juan Hernandez
Grade 3, Kimball Elementary
Poet-Teacher: Glory Foster
Teacher: Bene Calderon

"UFOs"
Lamson J. Nguyen/Grade 6/Horace Mann Middle

Talking Crafts

The European crafts pounding and rocking,
with palms open as he recalls simple victory.

The African craft sends a shocking message
about his design in movement: running
streams blessed with freedom.

He asked, "Have you ever of thought about
the weight of the night
or the stars of escape?"

> **Kelly Bennett**
> Grade 7, Pauma School
> Poet-Teacher: Brandon Cesmat
> Teacher: Coy Johnston

Ode to a Limpet Shell

Oh, limpet you are
a shiny gold twilight
sparkling
like a colorful jewel.
You are a yellow-orange
mountain
as slippery as ice
and as solid as a rock.
You look like a shark's jaw
or like a volcano.
You are a silver palace.
Oh, limpet you are
an immense brain
of the universe.

> **Scott Linger**
> Grade 4, Canyon View Elementary
> Poet-Teacher: Glory Foster
> Teacher: Renie Martin

Two Worlds

My name is Sarah Marie Sifton.
Of that I am sure,
But of other things,
I am not sure.
My mom thinks of me as a wild filly,
Unruly and hard to handle.
But the opinions of others?
I live in two worlds.
In one, I know what I am doing,
But the other is a constant mystery.
In one, I have friends,
But in the other
All friendship has ceased.
In one world, I am bold and speak my mind.
In the other, I am as quiet as a ghost.
In one, I feel as carefree and light as a bird.
In the other, I am restricted
And chained to a wall of silence.
Sometimes I forget which is which:
The world where I am somebody,
The other, where I'm as invisible as the atmosphere.

Sarah Sifton
Grade 5, Hawthorne Elementary
Poet-Teacher: Celia Sigmon
Teacher: Jim Riley

"Best Friends"
Aaron Toledo/Grade 12/Morse High

Sometimes Rough, Sometimes Mellow

My sister is like
a ladybug spreading her wings
when she jumps rope.
She is like the beach--
sometimes she's rough
like a great billowing storm.
Sometimes she's mellow
like a gentle calm sunset.
My sister is like a mountain
standing proud and tall.
She looks like she has chicken pox
because of all the freckles on her nose.
She is like an oval--
she goes away but
always comes around again.
My sister is like a pestle
crushing me when I'm mean to her.
That is my sister,
sometimes rough,
sometimes mellow.

Carly Rask
Grade 6, Valle Lindo Elementary
Poet-Teacher: Glory Foster
Teacher: Pat Neill

"Looking Into The Future"
Tsubasa Yamaguchi/Grade 8/Standley Middle

I Saw Andi

I saw Andi
on her front porch,
looking for someone
to play with
in the late afternoon
in June.
She looked like a flower
going to die but
when she saw me,
she opened.
All she wanted was
to play with me.

Molly Boyne
Grade 4, San Pasqual Union
Poet-Teacher: Brandon Cesmat
Teacher: Wendy Snapp

Art Gallery

My face is an art gallery,
Monet's lily pads drift in my brown eyes.

Downstairs, in my mouth,
Mona Lisa's sitting on my tooth easel.

Artists are in my hair,
Painting until the paint turns gray.

Painters warm up by
Trying the red paint on my rosy cheeks.

Finally bedtime comes.
Closing time is here.

People leave, eyelid doors close.

Marisa Luber
Grade 4, La Jolla Elementary
Poet-Teacher: Jana Gardner
Teacher: Barbara Rodenrys

Nasty Icky Lima Beans

Nasty icky lima beans taste
like terrible words
like on the nasty talk show Jerry Springer.
And then those very sad people jump up
and out of their chairs and
beat the living lima beans out of each other.

Collier Jones
Grade 4, San Pasqual Union
Poet-Teacher: Brandon Cesmat
Teacher: Victoria Young

My Brother Looks Like A Snail

Slimy, icky, gooey
and very, very slow.
He doesn't crow
he doesn't throw.
My brother
looks like a snail.
Little mouth, little head,
no teeth, no feet,
just crawl, crawl, crawl. . . .

Erika Rodriguez
Grade 6, Valle Lindo Elementary
Poet-Teacher: Glory Foster
Teacher: Pat Neill

Mike

If he were a tornado
he would suck me in and
take me for the wildest ride
spying on Indians and buffaloes
running like shooting stars
hitting Jupiter with a bang.
He would call from the sky
and take me away to the places
I dreamed of.
He would launch me around
like the wildest roller coaster
with no seats, no belts, and no rules.
He would flip me, row me, throw me
and at last he would dump me back
into the wild plains.
Then in the blink of an eye
disappear into the night sky
reflecting the night stars.

John Zhang
Grade 5, Torrey Pines Elementary
Poet-Teacher: Steve Garber
Teacher: Anna Lewis

"Reflection"
Adrian Reyes/Grade 10/Morse High

"Burning Heart"
Emily Clark/Grade 8
Bonita Vista Middle

Red Comes From The Heart

Red is the sound
of the devil's roar.
Red is the feeling
you get from danger.
Red is the fire
coming from your heart.
Red is the light
burning from your eyes.
Red tastes like blood
from your heart.
Red smells like cinnamon
yet is as sweey
as an apple.

Salvador Arroyo
Grade 3, Lincoln Acres Elementary
Poet-Teacher: Glory Foster
Teacher: Diane Horowitz

Love's Many Shapes

I love my dad, he is a crystal
shinning in the sun.
Sometimes he looks like
a rock, a ring, a pine cone
or an eye watching over me.
Sometimes he looks like an animal,
a bunny when he's sweet
or a tiger when he's mad.
I love him so much
I will do anything for him.
My dad is a shiny crystal.

Angela Raimondi
Grade 3, Palmer Way Elementary
Poet-Teacher: Glory Foster
Teacher: Melissa Harley

My Grandma and Grandpa

My grandma
wears Hope's dress
because my grandpa is dying.
I don't know
what to say to grandma.
She remembers when they were young
and went to Las Vegas to see the shows
and play the slots or blackjack.
Now, she longs to do it again
with him...for all eternity.

Danielle Hove
Grade 6, Ira Harbison Elementary
Poet-Teacher: Glory Foster
Teacher: Linda Cartwright

Blue Monkey Sipping Soda

I am a blue monkey climbing
on trees and bushes in the spring.
I am a circle drinking Pepsi
and eating enchiladas.
I am a Saturday night dancing
to my favorite bands like 98% and N'Sync.
I am eleven stars
twinkling in the night sky.
I am a child with a lollipop.
I am a blue jay sitting on a twig
on the banks of a river.
I am a girl with her first doll
squeezing it tightly.
I am Shaq shooting for the final basket.
I am Mia Hamm scoring a goal.
I am Mars just spinning in the universe
looking at the black sky.
I am me...A blue monkey!

Shannon Mockler
Grade 6, Ira Harbison Elementary
Poet-Teacher: Glory Foster
Teacher: Linda Cartwright

Hate

Hate is a dump
where you dump
what you hate

an electric guitar
being played loudly
all day long

a dog ripping apart a shoe
his eyes flashing rage

demons released to perform evil deeds.

Jorge Martinez
Grade 10, Chula Vista High
Poet-Teacher: Johnnierenee Nelson
Teacher: Jonathan Barns

"Gohan"
Rolando Herrera/Grade 10/Crawford High

Blinding Yellow

I have yellow hate so strong and bright
it blinds my eyes. I can't see anything,
but my sister sees me and says, "Monica,
stop pretending you're blind."
"I'm not pretending," I say and then
bump into a wall and it hurts,
a red baseball hitting my head.
My sister laughs and jumps away to tell our mother.

Monica Navarro
Grade 3, San Pasqual Union
Poet-Teacher: Brandon Cesmat
Teacher: Kim Read-Smith

"Morning Glory"
Kelly Thornton/Grade 7/Mesa Verde Middle

The Spoiling of an Aging Kiwi

His body old and soft to the touch
the color of his skin grayish-brown
his wooden rocking chair creaks as
he rocks back and forth
shedding small, thin, black hairs
on the seat.
His arms and legs sprout
small, curly black hairs that tickle
as they brush against your skin.
He has long hairy toes
hair coming out of his ears, his nostrils
he's quiet and speaks little.

In his eyes I see a lively waterfall
with rocks on its banks covered in green moss
once a bright vibrant thing
rich, ripe, and vigorous in his youth
now he grows near
to rotting in the earth--
grows dry.

Now I must leave him alone
must let him be
must let the spoiling of age
swallow him whole
and spit out the pit
that was once his soul.

Alegria Vicencio
Grade 8, Bonita Vista Middle
Poet-Teacher: Johnnierenee Nelson
Teacher: Casey Handrop

The Color of Humiliation

Humiliation is a neon sigh flashing in the dark.
It is a high note sung in the wrong place.
Humiliation is a lone tree on a prairie
at which everyone points and stares.
It is a lump, on an otherwise smooth surface.
Humiliation is a street corner
jutting out into a street
Humiliation is a branding iron, burning in and in.

Danielle Torre
Grade 8, Bonita Vista Middle
Poet-Teacher: Johnnierenee Nelson
Teacher: Casey Handrop

The Way I Like It

Red is a fire truck
that makes me feel like a stop sign,
like summer, heating the day.
Red makes me feel like the lines
on a board that separate the states.
It takes me to the sun
and brings me down like nothing.
Red is me,
the color of love and danger,
and that's the way I like it.

Jenny Meza
Grade 5, Lincoln Acres Elementary
Poet-Teacher: Celia Sigmon
Teacher: Susan Braden

"Ready to Battle?"
Kevin Lowe/Grade 8/Horace Mann Middle

Anger

Anger is like a knife
cutting through the sun
it is an island
coceived in a sea of hate

anger is a flower
losing all of its petals
a rabbit attacking a fox
that has just destoryed its home

anger is a battle
between your mind and your heart
your mind, the power of reason
but heart, the power of love

Alberto Corona
Grade 8, Bonita Vista Middle
Poet-Teacher: Johnnierenne Nelson
Teacher: Casey Handrop

My Friend, the Red M&M

My friend is like a Christmas tree
Always beautifully dressed
Like a salt shaker
Moving and shaking up our lives
Like chocolate
Sweet and a pleasure to have anytime
Like a bee
Buzzing around and stinging me with laughter
Like an eye
Looking at things differently
Like a nose
Always sniffing out and knowing other lives
My friend is a red M&M in a blue M&M world
Different...

B. B. Villanueva
Grade 7, Mesa Verde Middle School
Poet-Teacher: Glory Foster
Teacher: Terry Heck

"Best Buds"
Justine Keovoravongsa/Grade 4/Canyon View Elementary

My Busy Home

      In the kitchen
you hear tacos sizzling in the pan.
      You taste the red rice
savoring it in your mouth.
      You feel the heat
touching your hands.

      In the living room
go sit on the couch
      watch TV or lay on the floor
and play video games.
      Sleep in a chair
when you are sick.

      In my parent's bedroom
there's soft music playing
      parents sleeping.
there's snoring
      from a sleeping father.
The shower running
      making parents smell and look good.

      In my brother's room
toys lying on the floor
      never getting cleaned up.
There's a train set
      running nicely, a brother
sleeping soundly with his teddy bear.

Ashlee Corona
Grade 4, Canyon View Elementary
Poet-Teacher: Glory Foster
Teacher: Carl Bogucki

Green Fire

Kiwi, bright and green
an emerald forest
burning with light

I know it is young
sour, unripe
but kiwi is mischievous

I want to eat it
knowing how sweet it can taste
Kiwi laughs at my weakness
I take a bite

The flower stings my tongue
burning its tip with a whip of
green fire

Graciano Avalos
Grade 8, Bonita Vista Middle
Poet-Teacher: Johnnierenee Nelson
Teacher: Casey Handrop

Flower

A burst of crimson
burns outside my
window
with tongues of
flame
leaping from
the white-hot
center

Katherine Ramos
Grade 10, Torrey Pines High
Poet-Teacher: Jim Milner
Teacher: Marie McKittrick

"The Most Beautiful Flower"
Diana Thai/Grade 6/Horace Mann Middle

"Why Be Normal?"
Leslie Meredith/Grade 8/Bonita Vista Middle

Toilet

I sit. I read.
It sounds like a small ocean
with the waves crashing the rocky cliff.
When I'm sick, I hug it.
I like how the pot curves
and it looks like a giraffe with a long neck.
The seat looks like a lion's mane
or a plain white necklace.
The toilet is great!
The tank looks like a solid white aquarium
but no real fish are there,
only the spirits of the dead flushed ones.

Justin Scholey
Grade 6, Lewis Middle
Poet-Teacher: Tamara Johnson
Teacher: Jamie Walsh

Silver Scales

The rhino is silver with scales like a snake's.
He has horns that feel like rocks.
He is made of silver and is strong
like a knight in armor.
It charges for the attack and lowers its head
and hits a rock. Kaboom!
He makes a hole like an ax does.
His scales cling and clang and then
he falls apart.
I take the silver scales and bury them.

Eric Paarman
Grade 3, San Pasqual Union
Poet-Teacher: Brandon Cesmat
Teacher: Kim Read-Smith

The Pomegranate

Like the leathered face of a wise old man
the imperfect bumps and curves
of the round fruit
with spots of red and brown
swirled together
to make a fiery crimson globe.

When the knife goes in
a bloodyish liquid
spurts a Picasso-like painting
onto the napkin.

William Franklin
Grade 8, Bonita Vista Middle
Poet-Teacher: Johnnierenee Nelson
Teacher: Casey Handrop

I Am

I am
a balloon
flying free,
like a
book
flipping
a
hundred
pages
a
minute.
I am
a whale
migrating in the winter, a pool of gold coins.
I am a child running free
as a
wild colt,
a building
full of strange
animals with
a horn on each nail, with teeth of stars
and a ruby for a heart.

Allister Caluza
Grade 4, Mason Elementary
Poet-Teacher: Jana Gardner
Teacher: Jody Neiss

Shoelaces in Love

My shoelaces are in love.
They are tied in a knot.
They are stuck together forever,
or at least until the end of the day.

When I put on my shoes,
The Shoelace Inn,
another couple are stuck together.
My shoelaces are in love.

Tessa Miller
Grade 4, Spreckles Elementary
Poet-Teacher: Tamara Johnson
Teacher: June Pressler Pecchia

"Angel"
Brittany Estrada/Grade 8/Bonita Vista

A World of Living Color

There was
darkness
no light
no color
I picked up
my rainbow paints
my brushes the color
of the Caribbean parrots
I create. . .
Darkness becomes
light and color
reds of blood and heart
yellow of warm sunshine
blues and greens
of the plants, ocean and sky
become me too. . .
Living colors
The blues of rivers
and a sunny sky
opens my eyes
the red berries
are my lips
allowing me speech. . .
Yellow sun
brown dirt
drip and spread
forming my skin
I paint myself
coming to life
creating the colors
of my world
forever. . . .

Sandy Chan
Grade 7, Mesa Verde Middle
Poet-Teacher: Glory Foster
Teacher: Joie Nolasco

Rattlesnake

I saw a rattlesnake crawling in the dirt with its cascabel rattling.
When he sees me in total sight, his eyes are so dark, red and green.
He's green! Such wonderful colors on his wonderful skin.
He moved slowly like a shadow when I moved.
It was a dark afternoon on the ranch where I live.
Everyday I go walking, and wherever I go
that snake is always there, just being like my shadow beside me.

Victoria Fonseca
Grade 4, San Pasqual Union
Poet-Teacher: Brandon Cesmet
Teacher: Wendy Snapp

"The Meadow of Life"
Jeremy Peterson/Grade 7/Mesa Verde Middle

Fixing The Car

My father's hands
are greasy and oily
from working on his car
in the garage.
He is using a ratchet
and he asks me
to hand him a tool.
I get it and he says,
                    "*Thank you.*"

His hands are like
black clouds on a rainy day.
I ask, "Dad what are you
fixing under the car?"
"It's not too far," he answers.

Alan Wells
Grade 3, Lincoln Acres Elementary
Poet-Teacher: Glory Foster
Teacher: Diane Horowitz

"The Dirt Devil"
Michael Tactay/Grade 6/Valle Lindo Elementary

The Donut Man

The donut man
always taking walks
to "Sunny Donuts"
and showing kids his magic tricks
like turning a rock into a quarter.
Him with his funky glasses
sometimes scaring people.
Him singing a song
knowing every word.
Him with his dressy shirts
tuxedo pants or jeans.
The donut man's wife
told me he cuts his jeans
into shorts and wears them
around the house.
His tiny eyes, wrinkled forehead
and church music which he always plays,
this is my funky, fun, weird grandpa!

Crystal Felix
Grade 6, Ira Harbison Elementary
Poet-Teacher: Glory Foster
Teacher: Linda Cartwright

Fresh Delicious Bread

fresh delicious bread
sprinkled with sesame seeds

3 pounds of roast beef
smothered with pepper sauce

lettuce and tomatoes
covered with thin barbecue sauce

the best sandwich in the world
covered with juice and flavor and

"Not Yours"

written all over

"Not Yours"

desire

my hands gripped the bread

my conscious said no

but my tongue said yes

> **Kendra Wesley**
> Grade 6, The Language Academy
> Poet-Teachers: minerva and Jim Milner
> Teacher: Helen Peterson

Memory Stain

If I loosened its grip on my
emotional jugular
I might be rid of a thin track
of pale skin, like a crop circle
tainted on the flesh that
paints my voice box
a silver sliver of two hours of
memories, worth something
bigger than I can name
hanging by a cheap dime-colored chain
from where I draw my fire
need it so badly like a
shot to the heart.

Gina Abelkop
Grade 11, La Jolla High
Poet-Teacher: Jill Moses
Teacher: Robin Visconti

Anger

Anger is a piano that's out of tune
Anger is a cactus that's stuck on you
Anger is a swamp yelling, yet no one hears
Anger is like a lion roaring and chasing you
Anger is your heart going thump, thump, thump.

Joseph Manglicmot
Grade 5, Valley Vista
Poet-Teacher: Johnnierenee Nelson
Teacher: David Casdan

Thirty Foot Waves
to my uncle Kevin Worrall

If he were a thick blue wall of mist
he would speak to me of climbing
effortlessly
across tall mountains
there terrifying animals live
beneath the rocks
he's speak of being
where no one has ever gone
suddenly
he would fly off the teetering rock
become the cold wet spray
sizzling off thirty foot waves
crashing over the sea
quickly the spray lifts
to the never-ending sky
which will never be seen agin

Carlos Mason
Grade 5, Torrey Pines Elemtary
Poet-Teacher: Steve Garber
Teacher: Anna Lewis

"A Peak for One"
Brian Adams/Grade 8/Muirlands Middle

Anything Else

Anything else but old pancakes
or rusty nails
or candy rappers
and smelly old socks
or dirty hair and
sweat in a baseball cap
or a counterfeit Chancy
and Charizard or Blastois..
Especially rolling eyeballs.
Anything but that.

Shayna Gianas
Grade 4, Gage Elementary
Poet-Teacher: Celia Sigmon
Teacher: Laurie Hill

Diving Into a Poem

Look beyond the poem's surface
Different meanings
Different feelings
Behind each one
They have a rhythm all their own
Like an orchestra playing a symphony
The words are the notes
Softly, adagio
To show sadness
Loudly, allegro
Expressing hatred and anger
Poems have depth
Unlike a shallow pond
One has to dive into it
To grasp the meaning
Of each poem
Each line a stepping stone

Marianne Samonte
Grade 10, Morse High
Poet-Teacher: Glory Foster
Teacher: Mary Scanlon

Honorable Mention

Bonita Vista Middle

Stephanie Albon, "Hairpin Turn"
Lara Balistreri, Untitled
Taylor Barnes, "Why Leopards Got Their Spots"
Danielle Bristow, "Questions?"
Katie Burlason, "The Caged One's Treasure"
Samantha Cayabyab, "The World"
Ariel Cuaresma, "My Family"
Nick Danforth, "Nick's World"
Jonathan Feria, "The Whistling Wind"
Karen Garza, Untitled
Glenn Gimutao, "Elements"
Ashley Hamilton, "My Family"
Kris Hatfield, "A Bad Day on a Three-Wheeler"
Ryan Horiye, "Anger"
Allison Kwan, "Questions Troubling the Soul"
Andrew Mahler, "Before"
Greg Otero, "Pathway to Anger"
Michael Pilgrim, "Umm...."
Heather Silverio, "Why, Who, What, Where, When and How?"
Ashley Smith, "A World Where..."
Donald Snider, "Rage"
Emily Stroebel, "Temptation"
Jenny Tolentino, "What is Fear?"

Cadman Elementary

Robert Bunch, "Real Poetry"
Alex Fuller, "The Poetry Maze"

Canyon View Elementary

Luke Guo, "The Otter's Dream"

Central Elementary

Mary Cruz Arredondo, Untitled
Catherine Aylward, Untitled
Mariano Diaz, "Trumpet Shell"
Jose Espinoza, "Excitement"
Anthony Lopez, "My Mom's Kitchen"

Christina Lopez, Untitled
Maricela Pulido, "Happiness Seems Pink"
Nefi Varela, "Nintendo 64"

Charter School of San Diego

Trisha Berry, "Anger Controlling, Anger Creating"

Chula Vista High

Bryan Avalos, "The Brown Door"
Sonary Chhuon, "Loneliness"
Olga Gutierrez, "Living the Vida Loca"
Claudia Valle, "The Music Box"

Clairemont High

Marisa Lagos, "My Center" and "Why?"

Crawford High

Nhan Dinh, "Hands of Deception"
Raelynn Pili, "Shop Till You Drop"

Darnall Charter School

Tiffany Hurd, "Butterflies"
Erik Ovalle, "Family in the Rain"
Amelia Scott, "Hands"
Emanuel Zuniga, "Old Shoes"

El Toyon Elementary

Gener Banal, Jr., "If I Were a Balloon"
Gustavo Hanks, "Football Magic"
Natalhie Molina, "Running Bird"
Michael Saxour, "Bom Bom DJ"

Franklin Elementary

Anthony Contreras, "When Dark Skies Are Born"
Briana Schetter, "The Soul's Whisper"

Gage Elementary

Ryan Livingstone, "I Got the Golds"

Hawthorne Elementary

Chris Chee, "The Ice Cycle"
Alexander Lovell, "Display Case"
Ryan Luecke, "Technology"

Hearst Elementary

Efron Amberlicht, "Haircut"
Max Shulman, "My Weirdest Day"
Evan Weintraub, "Sparkling Butterflies"

Hoover High

Ignacio Alvarez, "I Used to Be"
Angel Garcia, "Secret"
Miguel Larios, "Fire"
Diana Romero, "A Place to Dream"
Lam Tran, "Hands"
Leizel Vergara, "Music of the Lyre"

Ira Harbison Elementary

Valerie Ann Abueg, "Stomach Growls"
Mark Eco, "Waterfalls and Dripping Salsa"

Jackson Elementary

Donnesha Brown, "Monkey"
April Guillemette, "Marker"
David Taing, "I Am"

Kimball Elementary

Ivan Cruz, "My Heart Is Poetry"

La Jolla Elementary

Lauren Shwisberg, "Dreams"

La Jolla High

Lin Faith, "Beach within a Shell"
Liu Yang, "To the People of the World"

Language Academy

Isaiah Blas, "The Mystery Me"
Jonathan Covarrubias, "Alcatraz"Tiffany Landaal, "Christina"
Denice Whittaker, "Orange Soda"

Las Palmas Elementary

Cristina Acosta, "My Gift to the World"
Jessica Felix, "If I Gave the Earth a Gift"

Lewis Middle

Kenneth Bosley, "Rage"

Lincoln Acres Elementary

Michelle Ceniceros, "Books"
Camille Galang, "Yellow's Song"
Isabel Gallo, "Painting My World"
Georgina Serna, "The Hand"

Lindberg/Schweitzer

James Cunningham, "Loneliness and Peace"
Jonathan D'Annes, "Inside a Book"
Chuck Diep, "Tree"
Rebecca Erbe, "Sun, Sun"
Tram Nguyen, "Tree"
Corey Wittman, "Soaring"

Longfellow Elementary

Mathew Arner, "Alternative"
Lauren Hinojosa, "Water"
Fortino Morales III, "I Wish for the Future"
Issac Oats, "The Eagles"
Gina Schmidt, "The Wind"
Eva Brione Valle, "The Forest"

Horace Mann Middle

Ben Baca, "204"
Sannara Chhoum, "The Glittering Kitchen"
John Hanna, "Lightening Dragon"

Leshawn Harris, "Recipe for Me"
Kevin Lowe, "Anger"
DeJon Parnell, "In the Shadow of Lies"
Hugh Pham, "A Piece of the World"
Sandra Ramirex, "My Heart Is a Cloud Burst"
James Thao, "Spring Breaks into Your Heart"
Sean Weigle, "My Grandpa Is a Maraca"

Marston Middle

Caty Frederick, "I Am the Colors"
Chelsea Johnson, "I Am a Whisper"

Mesa Verde Middle

Jared Braslawsky, "Remember"
Steven Burningham, "Mysteries from the Soul"
Jenna Carlisi, "Best Friend"
Janet Hwu, "Jack-In-the-Pulpit"
Rachel Neumann, "Cotton Candy, Churros and Pretzels"
Melissa Ocampo, "Violin"
Matt Rittmiller, Untitled
Michael Shinzaki, "Doomsday Asteroid"
Lindsay Warner, "My Second Home"
Jessica Wilcox, "The Storm's Symphony"

Morse High

Maria Diaz, "My Brother Is a Ruby Red 3000 GT Spyder"
Sherry Mae Eser, "In My Own Starry Night"
Jelynna Lizel Gomez, "Runaway, Runaway"
Benjamin Lawless, "Menagerie of the Book Covers"
Chien Le, "A Cushion of Clouds at the Edge of the Cliff"
James Mangapit, "Study for a Misguided Star"
Alex Martinez, "Sprouting Like Weeds"
Kenneth Phillips, "Love Grows through Hatred's Weeds"
Jenilee Quinto, "Jungle Jane=Hero"
Mina Sisouvong, "My Prince in Cotton Blends"

Muirlands Middle

Amanda Bacon, "If I Were a Leaf"
Susan Bell, "Flower"
Athena Haritatos, "Remember"
Brooke McSpadden, "My Cousin Danny"
Sindhura Reddy, "Beauty"

LaDocia Rose Schuetz, "The Orchard of Golden Fruit"
Natalie Snoyman, "Two A.M."

Palmer Way Elementary

Precious Falaminano, "Beautiful Painting"
Ernie Gutierrez, "My Waters"
Edgar Rodriguez, "Super Soccer"

Pauma School

Alondra Alba, "His Death"
Juan Almanza, "Star Marbles"
Therman Dixon, "To a River"
Flor Gomez, "Love Kick"
Nancy Gonzalez, "Old Dog House"
Sarah Letson, "Song or Spike"
Shanae Lofton, "Nevertheless Believing"
Buddy Matthews, "Draped Silence"
Lauren McGraw, "Nocturnal Confession"
Juan Carlos Rizo, "Cuetes y Cohetes"
Yessica Rizo, "Dad's Work"
Daniela Ruiz, "Mountains Listen"
Fabiola Ruiz-Ramirez, "The Electric Sun"
Carolina Velasquez, "Water Leaves"
Katie Wilson, "Bowl of Clouds"

San Pasqual Union

Sharilyn Baker, "Personality of Waves"
Lauryn Berner, "Ice Rain"
Christopher Boyne, "With Mom at the Park"
Ashley Hansen, "Millennial Fever"
Sanford Jackson, "Tree Brain"
Scott Johnston, "Mummy Dream"
Taylor Miligore, "Griddling Kitchen"
Mrs. J's Class, "Our Monster"
Alyssa Mueller, "Hate Sleeping"
Alexis Munoa, "Deep Water"
McKenna Plant, "Recognized"
Alejandra Quintero, "El Cochino"
Elizabeth Rockwell, "The Glory"
Leanne Ronk, "Drum Challenge" and "Tree Malediction"
Shamicka Simmons, "Moving Day"
Sarah Stewart, "Wiggle Colors"

Brandon Wilson, "Blue Stage"
Ian Wilson, "War Pencil"

SCPA

Emily Adamson, "Impressions"
Kaylyn Johnson, "Dreaming"
Erin Konishi, "I Believe"

Spreckels Elementary

Gregory Hawkes-Robinson, "Magnet Pantoum"
Jonica Johnson, "When I Am in Joyful Moods"

Standley Middle

Octavio Barranco, "The New Neighborhood"
Matthew Chambers, "Back to the Future Past"
Adam James Decker, "Things Inside Things"
Lisl Esherick, "The Taste of Time"
Lisa Hampton, "A Linked Pantoum"
Kathryn Jacoby, "The Rise of the Downtrodden"
Tyler Moselle, "Pantoum of Emerald World Horses"
Scotti Norman, "Waves of Darkness"
Linda Nyberg, "I Am What I Am"
Mackenzie Ooms, "Back Then"
Cary Robbins, "The Ball Playing Pantoum"
Tina Utter, "Path of Love"
Jimmy Zengel, "Black Winter"
Hua Zhao, "Reaching for the Future"
Blane Goodrich, "Not Even Thinking"

Torrey Pines Elementary

Michelle Gnanaratnem, "I Believe"
Austin Miller, "If I Were a Caterpillar"
Rachel Pedowitz, "Left Side Shoe"
Jacqueline Vinson, "If I Were an Owl"
Stephanie Nicole Vinson, "Our World"
Susan Wright, "It's True"

Torrey Pines High

Annie Foucault, "The Darkness"
Deema Saad, "These Teeth"
Lara Stapley, "Glistening Moon"

University City High

Belinda Gu, "Past the Stars and Beyond" and "Lost"
Gwen Kirby, "A Moment Not Wasted"

Valle Linda Middle

Fernando Hernandez, "A Shining Example"
Joshua Jo, "I Am Unique"
Nicholas Perez, "Heart Like an Eagle"
Chris Phelps, "Skate Boarding"
Abigail Santos, "Strong as the Ocean Breakers"
Ronald Veloria, "Greenest of Them All"

Valley Vista Elementary

Vance Apostol, "Fire on Ice Future"
Brittany Balderston, "My Difficult Life"
Elias Castro, "My Animal"
Michael Chambers, "Summer Is Hot"
Bryan Garlejo, "Poetry"
Henny Harrington, "The Moment"
Stephanie Herrera, "My Imaginary Painting"
Alberto Loaiza, "Poetry"
Isaac Murillo, "Poetry Means"
Jessica Resendez, "Imaginary Painting"
Armando Yee, "I Like To Feel Poetry"
Denise Yee, "When I Think about the Future"

Wangenheim Middle

Amanda Lee Barber, "Glass"
Lesset Ramos, "Inside and Out"
Stephen Sampson, "An Ode to Baseball"

Zamorano Elementary

Sarah Cooper, "The Sunset Stone"
Harold Pier, "Rock of Ages"